CW00459155

Contents

Chapter 1

Once Upon A Time

All children have a favourite bedtime story. Whether it's a classic fairytale or a modern Disney interpretation, there's no better guarantee of a peaceful night's sleep than a familiar tale told by a familiar face. Young Jennifer Aniston was no different. Except she preferred to eschew the standard scripts in favour of real-life retellings. For Jennifer, fact was far more interesting than fiction.

'Mom,' called Jennifer, gently creaking open her parents' bedroom door.

Stirred by the movement, Nancy Aniston sat up in bed. Squinting in the darkness, she could just make out the figure of her daughter illuminated by a splash of neon from the streetlamps outside. 'What's the matter, honey?' she yawned, slowly settling into consciousness.

'I can't sleep,' mumbled the woeful four-year-old, turning her toes inwards and cocking her head to one side.

Nancy had seen this performance before. She knew what was coming next. 'Do you want me to read you a bedtime story, sweetie?'

As if on cue Jennifer lifted her head and flashed a smile that could eclipse every streetlight in LA.

'And let me guess,' continued Nancy, an old hand at this game. 'You want to hear the one...'

'...where you got me from the hospital,' beamed Jennifer.

'The year was 1969 and we were all excited about a new arrival in the family,' Nancy began, as she tucked Jennifer into bed. 'We were very impatient and kept pestering the doctor for news on when we could collect our new baby. That day finally came on 11 February. Two hours after we arrived at the hospital, we walked out with our new baby girl. When Daddy came to pick us up, the nurses carefully placed the tiny pink bundle in my arms for the wheelchair ride out. When the elevator doors finally opened, we were greeted by smiling relatives. Big brother Johnny, who was eight at the time, rushed forward and thrust a bouquet of flowers towards me. Unable to speak, he touched his new sister on the cheek.

'As we climbed into the car, I handed our tiny bundle over to Daddy. He froze with fear, shocked by the fragile and delicate creature in his arms. We took the 101 freeway from Hollywood to our home in the Valley, the Californian sun sparkling on the windscreen. He refused to drive above 30 miles per hour and we stopped at every on-ramp. Nothing was gonna happen to his new baby!'

At that moment, Jennifer started to giggle. She imagined all the other cars beeping at Daddy to hurry up.

After allowing her daughter a moment for thought, Nancy continued, 'When we finally arrived home, Daddy carried our baby into the nursery and put her in a cradle. But Johnny insisted his new little sister sleep in his bedroom. He reckoned that, as he was the fastest runner in school, he could get to Mommy immediately if anything happened. He would keep a close guard and monitor every sound she made.

'True to his word, he would rush into the bedroom several times in one night demanding that I come and take a look. But, every time, I would walk in to find her still sleeping. Desperate to catch some sleep, I explained that babies usually let out a loud cry when they needed feeding. There was no chance we'd miss that!

'Whether it was helping change a diaper or passing me a blanket, Johnny was always eager to help out. He hated going to school, convinced that I wouldn't be able to cope alone. Stifled yawns and black circles under his eyes were telltale signs that he'd hardly slept all night. Finally, I allowed him to skip school and suggested he go back to bed. The poor thing slept all day! That night, we moved the cradle to the nursery and Johnny didn't offer a word of protest.'

Sad the story had come to an end, Jennifer demanded her mother tell it again.

'It's getting late, honey,' sighed Nancy. 'Remember what happened to Johnny when he didn't get his sleep? There's plenty more time for telling stories.' With that, she kissed her daughter on the forehead, switched out the light and retired to her own bedroom.

Given Jennifer's family background, it's hardly surprising she ended up working in the entertainment industry. Both her parents had Hollywood connections and, for a while, her dad John even struck gold with a role in the hit soap *Days Of Our Lives*. Born in Crete, his family moved to America and opened a diner in Eddystone, Pennsylvania. Jennifer's grandma remained in that same house until she passed away at the age of 94.

'She was the godmother, the centre of the family and amazingly strong,' says Jennifer with family pride. 'She had the most beautiful skin, the softest thing you ever felt, which I always attribute to her rubbing olive oil on it.'

Although now living in America, the Anastassakis clan upheld their Greek traditions. 'Greek mothers really take care of their men, and my father was her only son. He could do no wrong in her eyes,' smiles Jennifer. 'I probably shouldn't say this, but they say, "Never marry a Greek man, because he'll always expect you to wait on him!"'

However, John soon decided to ditch his tongue-twister of a surname in favour of something more user-friendly. For years, Jennifer believed her father had stumbled upon the name Aniston while driving through the city of the same name. Today she stands corrected.

After reading the anecdote in a magazine interview, a confused John called up his daughter to set her right. 'Where on earth did you get that story from, honey?' he asked her. 'It's nonsense.'

To this day, the origins of the Aniston family name remain a puzzle.

Jennifer recalls her father was 'a strikingly handsome man... with a moustache'. As he towered over the small child at six feet two inches, she looked up to him as a 'gentle giant'. 'He's one of the nicest men you'll ever meet... unbelievably shy and funny!' she would later tell reporters.

An American through and through, Nancy Aniston grew up in New York in a family of five sisters. At the age of 12, however, she was devastated to learn her mother had deserted the household. Permanently scarred by the experience, she would refuse to discuss the matter in later years.

After moving to California, Nancy landed a job at Universal film studios. Although desperately seeking the limelight, she started out faking autographs for Rock Hudson! But it wasn't long before her good looks caught the eye of casting directors. 'My mom is gorgeous, a pretty thing, so men hired her,' explains Jennifer.

Her early roles included a stint on *The Red Skelton Show* and *The Beverly Hillbillies*. A young Jennifer would describe her mum as 'very warm, loving, nurturing, wise'.

Nancy was just 24 years old when she met John, but already had a three-year-old son from a failed teenage marriage. Struggling to make ends meet, she was working as a model. She was struck by John's good nature and his strong family values. Three years after their first date, the couple married in 1965. But life wouldn't be easy. Although an experienced actor with collegiate training,

John spent most of his time out of work. Ironically, Nancy was experiencing an upsurge in her career, which put an inevitable strain on the relationship. Nancy set to work on revamping her husband's appearance in the hope a new look would help him land more roles.

Desperate for a short-term cash injection, John undertook some part-time work as a door-to-door salesman. But his move into real estate was ill fated. A slump in the housing market left John despondent and he gave up.

'Perhaps you should find a more stable source of income?' Nancy suggested tentatively, careful not to knock John's pride.

'What's the point?' he sighed. 'If I take up a regular job, I can wave goodbye to an acting career once and for all!'

And so the family continued to live by meagre means. Every day, Nancy would return home from modelling jobs to find her husband slumped in front of the TV. Biting her lip, she fought back any irritation. After all, John would have given his right arm to swap places with her. But, when Nancy found out she was pregnant, a decision had to be made. Reluctant to compete with her husband any longer, she gave up acting and chose to concentrate her efforts into being a full-time mother instead.

'She didn't think she was a good actress and quit,' Jennifer would later tell reporters. 'What she wanted was to have a family.'

Accepting a loan from Nancy's father, the couple moved into a larger house. Although dilapidated, they set to work on transforming the property on a shoestring budget. Unable to afford new furniture, they scoured the streets for second-hand items. Bringing up a baby in a partial building site wasn't easy. Nancy would later tell stories of how her newborn daughter would reach out from her crib and pull at pieces of faded sunflower wallpaper. Amused by the habit, she never once intervened. She preferred to interpret it as Jennifer's own little contribution towards renovations.

'I think I'm just someone who didn't enjoy wallpaper,' Jennifer later deduced. 'I prefer paint.' Even to this day, she steers clear of wallpaper. 'I think paints are much more interesting. The textures. Wallpaper is like a patch.'

One of Jennifer's earliest memories involved crawling over fake white brick tiling on her parent's new dining-room floor. 'I don't know why,' she says. 'I'm going somewhere. Going somewhere. Trying to get to the other side.'

For the first few years of her life, Jennifer didn't own a new item of clothing. Instead, her wardrobe consisted of hand-me-downs, passed on by family friends. Reluctant to leave their baby daughter at home, Nancy and John barely left the house. Besides, there was never any room in their budget for a social life. On one occasion, when they did accept an invite to a Hollywood party, Nancy recalls they only lasted an hour before they made a unanimous decision to return home. Years later, when Jennifer would question the sincerity of her father's affections, Nancy would use that story to prove otherwise.

Although John's career continued to stagnate, the couple still managed to move in Hollywood circles. Two of their closest friends were Lynn and Telly Savalas. A fellow Greek, Telly shot to fame in the TV programme *Kojak* and was associated worldwide with his catchphrase 'who loves you, baby?'. Instant friends, the two couples would regularly meet up for heated games of bridge. It was during one of these games that Telly brought up the subject of two-year-old Jennifer's baptism. As John's best man, according to Greek tradition, he was also in line to be Jennifer's godfather. An agreement was made and Nancy set to work on planning a traditional ceremony. Seeking instruction from her mother-in-law Mana, she learned Jennifer's clothing should be entirely removed during the ceremony and replaced with a new set from the godparents. Guests should also receive gifts of almonds and wheat berries sweetened with sugar and cinnamon.

On the day of the ceremony, Telly kept Jennifer quiet by whispering gently to her. He even persuaded her to sip the holy wine. Afterwards, guests were invited to a grand reception at the Savalases' home. Jennifer arrived in style in a Rolls-Royce. Unfortunately, the excitement proved too much and she vomited all over Nancy. Fearing the holy wine would be desecrated her grandmother insisted the soiled garments should be packed in plastic to take home. Later, she washed them in a tub and poured the dirty water into her rose garden, fearing the sacred fluid would be contaminated if poured down the sink. To this day, Jennifer is still amused by the story.

Throughout Jennifer's formative years, Telly was always on hand to support his godchild. 'I was close to

Telly when I was younger. He was just the coolest guy,' she coos. 'He'd send me lollipops in the mail and I remember on my seventh birthday he had a pink bicycle delivered to my door. He was one of those unbelievably generous human beings to his entire family, and there were a lot of them.'

Another male figure prominent in Jennifer's life was her half-brother Johnny Melick. Desperate to protect his little sister, he was never far from her side. On trips to the park, he would always make sure she had plenty of cool water to drink and quickly intervened if other children tried to do her harm. On one occasion, when Jennifer was four, she narrowly missed drowning when her tricycle careered into the swimming pool. 'Just bad gauging,' she shrugs at the memory. Thinking this must be some sort of game, her pet white poodle Dimitri quickly followed suit. Fortunately, Johnny wasn't far away. Without giving it a second thought, he dived into the pool to rescue his sister.

But, like any siblings, the pair would also fight. Johnny grew particularly fond of frightening Jennifer. 'Once, when we were young, he made me watch *Friday the 13th*, after which I went into the bathroom. He'd snuck in there first and hid behind the shower curtain, then jumped out, wearing this horrible mask that had eyeballs falling out and snakes for hair. I let out a scream and… Well, let's just say it was a good thing I was sitting on the toilet.'

'From very early on, it was evident Jennifer had a vivid imagination,' Johnny recalls. 'From the minute she popped out, she was the queen of make-believe. She was always walking her Barbies through scenes. And later, when she started watching TV, she was the Bionic Woman.'

Jennifer had two particular favourite dolls; one was a Barbie head with hair you could brush and a face to apply make-up and the other was a Cher doll with long black hair and high heels.

'I was obsessed with high heels when I was little!' she gushes. 'I'd create a whole apartment complex from shoeboxes, and toilet paper for curtains. The Cher doll was a tall doll... thank God, my dad had big feet.'

Years later, as a famous adult, Jennifer would meet the superstar singer. Quite wisely, however, she never mentioned the doll. 'I think there are some things that are just better left unsaid.'

On another occasion, Nancy found her daughter laughing hysterically and rolling around on the floor. 'What's so funny?' asked Nancy, quite confused.

'I'm playing with the Little People,' replied Jennifer to a question that seemed stupidly obvious.

'Oh,' Nancy responded, none the wiser.

For the next hour-and-a-half, Jennifer sat playing with her new group of friends, invisible to the naked adult eye. Each day, she would return to the same spot in the dining room to see the Little People. Her fits of laughter always gave the game away.

While John and Nancy accepted their daughter's eccentricities as relatively harmless, family friends feared the young child's grip on reality was dangerously loose. Her grandmother even tried to wean Jennifer away from the make-believe playmates with a family of cloth dolls.

Unfortunately, her ploy didn't quite go to plan. Although Jennifer fell instantly in love with her new toys, she couldn't wait to share them with the Little People.

Eventually, however, Jennifer's dreams were shattered when her father accidentally trampled her invisible friends to death. Desperate to console his daughter, John pretended to pick up the Little People and nurse them back to health. Jennifer finally calmed down, although John helpfully suggested it might be a good idea if they put the Little People in the bathtub to avoid any future mishaps. Jennifer agreed and they carefully transported the Little People to a new home. That was the last anyone heard of them, much to John and Nancy's relief. Speaking about the incident today, Jennifer recalls very little. 'Perhaps my mother made it up,' she laughs. 'Let's make her think she's crazy! That will guarantee she'll become an actress.'

Although John was still determined to pursue a career in acting, he slowly came to the conclusion that he might need to earn money by a different means. At Nancy's suggestion, he went back to college and studied medicine. The family upped sticks from Los Angeles and moved to Eddystone just outside Philadelphia, where John's Greek relatives lived.

But an even greater move was on the horizon, when John was forced to leave the country. 'He was too old to get into universities here, so we moved to Greece for a year when I was five,' explains Jennifer. She has vivid memories of her time spent in Athens. 'I have the most amazing memories... a bin of oranges that sat in the living room and the cat that lived on our terrace.' Quickly acclimatising to her new surroundings, Jennifer started to learn Greek. Today, however, she can hardly speak a word of the language. 'For the most part, it's just staring at a bunch of mouths moving.'

But, after just 12 months abroad, the phone call John had been waiting for finally came. Producers of a new daytime soap, *Love of Life*, were holding auditions. John's agent reckoned he'd be ideally suited to one of the roles. Sure enough, after an initial audition, he was called back for a screen test and landed the part of Edward Aleata. The family gathered up their belongings and moved to Manhattan.

Unprepared for the culture shock, it took Jennifer some time to adjust to city life. She wasn't used to crowds of people waiting to cross the road or vagrants curled up in shop doorways. But she still considers her childhood memories of New York to be her happiest. 'Those were my best times as a kid,' she smiles. 'I can remember this one party we had. Maybe 15 of my parents' friends were over, scotch in their glasses, or sherry. I'm not sure if I belly danced for everyone that night, but I used to cut a real mean one for my Greek relatives. I used to sing, too – in the car, in front of the mirror, anywhere. I was about seven and absolutely fearless. I remember playing charades with the grown-ups that night, and all the laughter. Then it was time for me to go to bed, but you could never put me down when there was a good time to be had. Again and again, I tried to sneak out of my bedroom toward the happy sounds, but they kept making me go back until I was exhausted and fell asleep.'

During this period, the Aniston household was a happy one. A shadow of economic hardship had finally been lifted and raised voices were replaced with peals of laughter. 'My dad had this laugh that made you want to laugh,' says Jennifer. 'He still does. Same with my mom. When one would start, the other would follow. My mom's face would get red and her eyes would start watering and her vocal cords would close up, and it would be so funny that you'd be swept up in it and then you couldn't stop. There's nothing better than contagious laughter. It's the most peaceful feeling in the world.'

At the time, Jennifer couldn't fully appreciate her father's growing fame and success. 'I didn't really remember much. When you grow up with it, it's just Daddy's job. It was all just people and pictures and flashes.' But she does recall an occasion when *Superman* star Christopher Reeve appeared on *Love of Life*. 'I remember being with my mother and running into him on the street, and I kept going, "Mom, c'mon! Let's go, let's go, let's go." And then, like, a week later we went and saw *Superman* and I was like, "Why did you let me run away?" And my mother was like, "Well, I tried…"'

After all their years of toil and struggle it seemed as if Nancy and John were finally reaping their well-deserved dues. Their bank balance ballooned and at last it appeared Jennifer would have everything she'd ever wanted. For the first few years at least, that was exactly how life panned out. But stormy times lay ahead. Very soon, Jennifer would find herself embroiled in a family trauma that would scar the happy-go-lucky child for the rest of her life.

Chapter 2

A Family Divided

For weeks Jennifer had been looking forward to her best friend's 11th birthday party. It had been the prime topic of conversation in class, and the night before the big event Jennifer could hardly sleep. As she lay in bed, wide-eyed, she imagined the many party games and wondered if she might be lucky enough to win a prize. Despite her mother's protests, Jennifer refused to fall asleep. Eventually, worn out by excitement, she drifted off.

The next morning, Nancy helped Jennifer gift wrap her present and dropped her off at the party. Kissing her daughter goodbye, she promised she'd be back later that afternoon at 4pm. The hours flew past and Jennifer was visibly disappointed when her mother finally returned. 'Please, Jennifer,' reasoned Nancy, as her daughter showed signs of a tantrum. 'I'm really not in the mood for this today.'

As she drove home, Nancy stared quietly into the distance. For the first time in five years, she picked up a cigarette and took a long drag. Sensing something must be wrong, Jennifer felt suddenly uncomfortable. Once they reached home, Nancy asked Jennifer to join her in the sitting room.

'There's something I need to tell you, Jennifer,' she sighed, hesitating to catch her breath. 'Daddy's been having some problems and he's not going to be around for a while.'

At first, Jennifer was confused, then she suddenly started to panic. A tear rolling down her cheek, she grabbed hold of Nancy and refused to let go. Jennifer describes the moment her family fell apart as the most painful experience of her life. 'She [Nancy] didn't say he was gone forever. I don't know if I blocked it, but I just remember sitting there, crying, not understanding that he was gone. I don't know what I did later that night or the next day. I don't remember anything other than it being odd that all of a sudden my father wasn't there. And he was gone for a while.'

It would be almost a year until Jennifer saw her father again. During that period, she didn't once hear from him. Two years earlier, Jennifer's half-brother Johnny had moved back to California to live with his natural father. 'He felt badly that I was left with the situation while he had the freedom to live his adult life.' At the time, Jennifer couldn't understand why he'd decided to leave. 'It never made sense to me. I didn't understand that. I mean, who is Johnny's other father? He must be my father too.'

From now on, Nancy and Jennifer only had each other to depend upon.

Eventually, it transpired that John had left Nancy for another woman. He'd been having an affair with one of his co-stars, whom he would eventually marry. Nancy was devastated when she found out and vowed to spare Jennifer the heartbreak. But, after a while, she grew tired of Jennifer's constant requests to see her father and resigned herself to telling the truth.

'When will Daddy be coming home?' asked Jennifer for the umpteenth time.

'He won't,' sighed Nancy, bracing herself for the inevitable. 'Your father's with someone else; he's not coming back.'

Jennifer was shocked. 'Mommy, I can't believe I'm going to be one of those kids who grows up without a father,' she wept.

Unable to deal with the situation herself, Nancy could offer her daughter little consolation.

'It was tough,' Jennifer recalls. 'Like any separation is tough. Your self-esteem and everything is sort of formed by your parents and, if that's not so stable, you're going to be a bit off-kilter. I started looking into all that in my early twenties, and I'm only realising now that I didn't do too well. It didn't feel great.'

Refusing to accept the truth, for a while, Jennifer even blamed herself for the separation and subsequent divorce. 'It was awful. I felt so totally responsible. It's so cliché, but I really felt it was because I wasn't a good enough kid.'

With hindsight, John admits the emotional

repercussions of his actions were tremendous. 'I knew the divorce was hard on her. And I'm sure I could have done a lot of things to make it easier, but it was very difficult.'

Mother and daughter slowly struggled to accept their new life. Alongside the obvious emotional strains, they also suffered serious financial problems. John had been the sole breadwinner in the household and kept a tight reign on the finances. In his absence, the family income sank dramatically. While Jennifer had been given a brief glimpse of a wealthy lifestyle, the future looked much more bleak. Money was now an issue and a serious one at that. Meals out became a rare treat and Jennifer was only ever allowed to order tap water. Trips to the theatre also ceased and Jennifer was often left to make her own entertainment. 'Since we didn't have a lot of cash, it was more, "Here are some dolls and crayons to play with."'

The experience obviously had a lasting impact on Jennifer and she vowed to be financially independent in later life. 'It made me one of those people who say, "I'm going to be completely self-dependent, because I don't want a relationship to be based on finances,"' says Jennifer. 'I couldn't wait to finally go out and make my own money. The idea of never relying on someone else always thrilled me. That way, what's going on between two people is strictly what each is bringing to the other: love, whatever. When you hear people say, "I can't leave because of money," I mean, dear God, I don't want any relationship to be about money. It's too corrupt.'

Overall, however, Jennifer remained fairly upbeat about her new situation. She and Nancy moved to an apartment on 92nd Street and Columbus Avenue. She admits city life required some adjusting. 'I attract lunatics,' she laughs. 'One time when I was in 11th grade there was this homeless guy on the street who looked just like Santa. Beard. Huge guy. Big gut. Everyone was walking by him, finding him all cute and charming. Then I come by and he slugs me across the face! And everyone else just keeps walking. Because, you know, nobody wants to get hit by Santa!'

And she loved the new apartment. 'At the time, it was pretty seedy,' she frowns. 'But for me it was amazing. We were on the 21st floor with a balcony and you could see the Empire State Building. It was in, like, a project, but it was beautiful. I wouldn't change anything. As much as I curse my parents at times, I also thank them for all of it!'

Unfortunately, Nancy wasn't quite so optimistic. Disappointed that her dream of a close-knit family had fallen apart, she couldn't quite move forward. 'She definitely had moments of bitterness,' admits Jennifer. 'Because she had nowhere to go. And that's hard to watch. I feel like, God, Mom, you were robbed of so much opportunity. If you could've had a voice in your ear saying, "Do what you want to do." But my mom liked the security of a traditional marriage, didn't mind being the wife with the husband bringing home the bacon.'

Living with Nancy wasn't easy. 'It was interesting,' sighs Jennifer. 'The good, the bad, and the ugly.' But, she adds diplomatically, 'We had a really good relationship. I wasn't the easiest kid. I was a smartass. I'm sure there was a lot of strain on her, since it was just she and I. Things were tough, and you always say, "God, I wish I did that differently." I wish I had been better as a teenager to my mom. But I'm kind of grateful for everything difficult that happened; it creates drive.'

It was a long time before John made any effort to contact his daughter. Feeling sheepish, he dreaded having to explain his actions to a child and preferred to avoid confrontation. He was convinced Jennifer would only resent him for leaving. In truth, Jennifer was desperately waiting for his call. 'My dad wasn't great with kids,' admits Jennifer. 'He loves kids, he loves me, but, you know, I've seen guys that are great with their daughters.'

Eventually, John plucked up the courage to pick up the phone. Twelve months had passed since he first walked out. In that time, he'd struck gold with a new role as Victor Kiriakis in the soap *Days Of Our Lives* and was a regular fixture in every American household but Jennifer's.

'Hey, Jennifer! How's it going?' asked John, his voice slightly trembling.

'Daddy?' replied Jennifer, unable to conceal her delight.

'Tell you what. How about I pick you up and we go and see *The Fantastiks* tonight?'

As promised, John picked Jennifer up and after dinner they went to see the show. During the meal, Jennifer asked why Daddy had decided to leave. Looking down at his food John started to mumble something about the marriage not working. As Jennifer recalls, he didn't explain himself particularly well. 'He's not a good communicator,' she says in his defence. Looking back at the marriage, she can agree that it wasn't working. 'Maybe if my parents had talked more... There were signs, but also, knowing my father, he probably didn't say anything. As best he could, he explained and apologised, and it's enough. We've made up. There are still parts that are hard for me, but I'm an adult. I can't blame my parents any more.'

After that initial meeting, John committed to visiting Jennifer more regularly. 'I started seeing him on weekends, and this new way of life just unfolded. He had a house in New Jersey. I'd go out on Friday nights, then come back on Sunday nights. My memories as a child are about just going place to place and taking care of adults.'

But John struggled to keep his promises. Between working and building a new relationship, he had little spare time to spend with his daughter.

For weeks, Jennifer had been preparing for her stage debut in the school play. She was playing a flower that bent in the wind. 'Mom, do you think Daddy will come?' she eagerly asked Nancy.

But, when the night of the performance finally came, John was conspicuous only by his absence. Peeping out from behind a curtain, Jennifer scanned the room. She repeated this action several times until every seat in the room was full. After the show, she ran over to Nancy and said, 'Daddy didn't come.'

Nancy didn't know what to say. 'We'll ask him to come again,' she said, hugging her daughter.

But on the second night of the show there was still no sign of John. Jennifer was crushed. Angry, Nancy picked up the phone and demanded an explanation. He'd better have a pretty good reason for breaking his daughter's heart!

'Oh, I forgot,' he replied.

'But I'm afraid she might think you don't love her,' pleaded Nancy.

John was clearly irritated by what he interpreted to be an overzealous interference. 'You don't know what you're talking about. She knows I love her.'

Unfortunately, Nancy *did* know what she was talking about. Over time, Jennifer started to believe her father simply didn't care. 'My dad didn't know how to be a great dad. I was a clown, and always sort of getting into trouble in school, and he thought I was a failure and stupid.' With hindsight, Jennifer understands that her father probably had no inkling of how disruptive his actions would prove to be in later life. 'I started to doubt myself,' Jennifer says sadly. 'The biggest gift he gave me was to say, "I'm sorry I wasn't there." He wasn't. He was bad. He wasn't a bad guy, but he was typical of his generation. Now he's a great dad.'

Tired of protecting her ex-husband, Nancy eventually revealed to Jennifer the real reason behind Daddy's sudden departure. She was fed up with bearing the brunt of responsibility for the divorce and wanted to set the record straight. Jennifer took the news calmly, but struggled to accept it was real. The truth only really hit home when Daddy decided to introduce his new girlfriend. Jennifer was visiting her grandma at the time. Her father walked into the front room and hurriedly removed every photo of Nancy he could find. His new girlfriend was waiting outside in the car and refused to enter the house until every picture had gone.

As much as Jennifer enjoyed spending time with her

father, her visits were often emotionally harrowing. Upset and confused, she had trouble expressing her feelings. One week, she returned home and slumped in the armchair. 'They're going to make me see a shrink to help me adjust,' she sighed.

Nancy reassured her daughter that it might be a good idea to speak with someone. But, after the first consultation, Jennifer rushed straight to her bedroom and refused to speak to anyone.

A further blow came when John announced that any physical contact between himself and Jennifer must stop. Jennifer had always been naturally affectionate, but John's new girlfriend considered so much hugging and kissing to be an unhealthy habit. Jennifer was distraught, especially when other little girls were allowed to hug their fathers. 'I wish my Daddy loved me like that,' she said, hanging her head.

The situation hit rock bottom when Jennifer returned home from a weekend break in floods of tears. 'Daddy said that from now on my weekend visits will be cut to every other week because he and his girlfriend need some weekends alone,' she bawled.

Jennifer had spent the previous few weeks visiting her father's new cottage close to a ski resort. In that time, she had become quite proficient on the slopes. 'Mommy, there are only three weeks left before they close the lift. Please can you talk him into waiting until the ski season is over so I can practise a little longer.'

Nancy promised to do her best, but had little success.

'I need to have time for my relationship,' insisted John.

'Jennifer knows I love her, but, sorry, the three remaining weekends of ski season are out of the question.' His decision was final.

Fearing he might leave again, Jennifer would do anything to please her father. Nancy found it painful to watch. 'Jenny would chatter on, trying to entice him to stay on the phone. He was a busy man who had to rush off and the hang-up always came far too soon. She'd flash a brave smile and run off to hide in her room. I never knew when to follow or when to leave her alone.'

But John wasn't the only person Jennifer was desperate to please. Unwittingly, Nancy was also exerting pressure on her daughter. Like any child involved in a divorce, Jennifer found herself at the centre of an emotional tug of war. She hated conflict and would do anything to resolve arguments between her estranged parents. 'My dad doesn't like to yell,' she says. 'And he's sort of calm about the way he has an argument. And I'm kind of like that mode of "Let's discuss it." My mom was always a little louder.'

Desperate to ease the tension, Jennifer would try to make light of situations. Like most comic performers, she honed her craft by dealing with a difficult childhood. 'I'd do funny things to try to bring back the laughter. It's hard to recall now what those things were. Maybe I've blocked them out. I guess I've learned to make a living doing what I did to try to heal myself as a kid.

'I was always the mediator,' she says. 'I was always trying to smooth things over and get everybody to laugh. I was constantly making sure everybody else was happy and feeling OK. I've definitely got elements of the good girl running through my veins. A lot of the time I felt like a middleman taking care of two children. It's a big responsibility to feel that you're in control of your parents' happiness. I'm slowly trying to let go of that resentment.'

Jennifer recalls the occasions when her parents would argue and her futile attempts to reconcile their differences. 'I'd talk to both of them. Sometimes I'd get in the middle and get really pissed off. You don't understand it when you're little; it's just what you do. But as an adult you can see that they were human and there was a divorce and another woman and there was Mother's jealousy and anger toward Dad and his anger toward Mom. What happens is you just don't want any conflict. That's the main thing: Try and keep everything calm. I'd try to be a good girl so that I didn't get in trouble.'

Today Jennifer admits that her childhood was complicated. 'I learned a lot about human relations and emotions at a young age, dealing with adults who were all of a sudden children. It's definitely hard. You deal with them fighting through you. That's a drag.'

The experience undoubtedly left her with emotional scars and insecurities that would take years to resolve. But, had she the power to turn back time, Jennifer is adamant she wouldn't change a thing. 'As painful and frustrating as it is, I wouldn't have wanted to grow up any other way. You can have a crappy childhood and grow up to let it completely overwhelm you or you can choose to be a fighter and say, "I'm not going to let that happen."'

Determined never to repeat the mistakes her parents had made, that's exactly what Jennifer did.

Chapter 3

Bitten by the Acting Bug

Given her parents' background in showbusiness, it was only a matter of time before Jennifer caught the acting bug. Signs of a career on the stage were evident from very early on. Games of make-believe offered a comfortable escape from reality and Jennifer quickly developed a skill for pretending to be someone else. Her decision to tread the boards may also have stemmed from a desire to please her father or even beat him at his own game. Her desire to become an actress was fully confirmed by a trip to the theatre. 'I went to see *Children of a Lesser God* on Broadway,' she says. 'I was sitting in the second or third row, and I was just so blown away and I walked out saying, "That's what I want to do."'

Aware of the industry pitfalls, John and Nancy had always been keen to steer their daughter in a different direction. Growing up, Jennifer wasn't allowed to watch much television. She never even watched her father on *Days Of Our Lives*. 'My mother didn't believe in television. I know it sounds silly, because my dad was on a daytime soap but I wasn't even allowed to go to the movies until I was 12!' Looking back, Jennifer thanks her mum for being so strict. 'It's something I want to do as a mother. We have that video thing now, where you pop a kid in front of a TV and they're like zombies. You should throw pencils and paper in their hands instead.'

When Jennifer was allowed to spend time in front of the box, she loved every viewing minute of it. 'I was allowed to watch *Donny and Marie* once in a while. That was my big treat!' Jennifer would sit on her bed and listen to TV shows she'd tape recorded. 'I'd play *Joanie Loves Chachi* and pretend I was Joanie and sing and all that stuff. We didn't have a VCR, so I used to sit by the TV with a tape recorder when it was on, and then go to sleep singing along with the theme song.' Jennifer also developed her first teenage crush on the lead character played by Scott Baio. 'I'd loved him from *Happy Days*,' she confesses. But John was quick to nip his daughter's obsession in the bud. 'He said, "You are not marrying Scott Baio!" Poor Dad, he took it so seriously.'

Part of her fascination with TV stemmed from escapism. 'I remember thinking, I'm going to get out of this house. Not that my house was a miserable place, but I was eager to be an adult. You're always so eager to be an adult, and then here you are, an adult, and, God, you wish you weren't.'

When she was 12 years old, Jennifer was sent to her

room for not being interesting enough. 'My father told me I had nothing to say,' she says. 'He made me leave the table.' From that moment, Jennifer was adamant she wanted to become an actress. 'I remember dreaming about being on TV.'

Jennifer admits childhood fantasies shaped her career as an actor. 'It was all I thought I could do. Maybe because of my childhood, I was escaping, I wanted to be a clown and to be happy... Actors are tortured children,' she explains. 'We're all just lost and vulnerable creatures who don't know who we are. I kind of feel like I've gotten away with something in that way because being funny is sort of what I did as a kid... and then all of a sudden I found a way to make a living at it. I thought I was going to be a serious actor... Realising that we can sort of just draw – it's just drawing from our own life – and how can we jump in. It's sort of fun to just play. The hardest thing is to sit right here and just be normal.'

Her goal, in those days, was to be a soap star. '*General Hospital* was my favourite,' she says, 'because their make-up was always perfect, and the hair, and the clothes – I loved that. Looking back, of course, I realise it wasn't a good thing. I was always reading those beauty magazines and wanting to become this unattainable thing. Then one day, you're in it – you're the girl in the pictures, and suddenly you realise it's all smoke and mirrors, airbrushing, lighting, stretching. No wonder people are killing themselves. Starving themselves. Popping pills. They're all trying to achieve something impossible.'

Despite her ambitions, John tried to dissuade Jennifer

from taking up acting. Having spent years out of work, he knew how tough the industry could be. He loved his daughter too much to see her go through a similar experience. There was no guarantee she would find the success she so desperately craved. 'If anything, my father tried to influence me the other way. He didn't think much of the business, especially for his daughter. He knew it could be cruel. It's so full of rejection.'

John agrees he was unhappy about the prospect. 'Well, I wasn't terribly thrilled,' he admits. 'I don't think a father who knows anything about this business would be thrilled to have a daughter who is in it... Why trust your kid into that? You try to protect them from all the bad people out there. In showbusiness, you get chewed up and spat out... I wanted her to go to college, and she just didn't want to. She was anxious to get on with it. Once she decided what she wanted to do, she was very driven.'

Jennifer's half-brother Johnny also showed some concern. 'Growing up, we saw our parents struggle,' says Melick. 'My father didn't really lock himself into a steady income until Jennifer was five. And we were all worried about her going through that.'

Their words fell on deaf ears. Spurred on by her father's doubting, Jennifer was desperate to prove him wrong. 'Part of me felt that he didn't believe in me, so there was a little bit of "I'll prove it to you!" He also didn't know how much I loved it.

Overall, Jennifer was determined to be successful and independent. 'I wanted to be self-sufficient. I wanted to have something of my own that I loved to do,' she says.

'So many of our parents and grandparents, the women especially, didn't have that. I was determined not to be chained to my home. I respect those people tremendously, but I know my mom would have been a happier person if she'd blossomed to her full potential. And you never get that time back. So I'm really trying to enjoy it. Can you imagine that feeling, to be 65 years old and to have missed whatever it is you've dreamed of?'

Keen to nurture her daughter's active imagination, Nancy eschewed the normal school curriculum in favour of a Waldorf education. Rather than focus on the traditional reading, writing and arithmetic, the emphasis was placed on developing a child's critical thinking and encouraging creativity. When the Anistons had moved to New York, Nancy chose to enrol Jennifer in a Rudolf Steiner school. She would have the same teacher and classmates for the first eight years. Nancy hoped this would give her troubled daughter some much-needed security.

At first, Jennifer struggled to settle in and make friends. As the new girl in town, she frequently bore the brunt of childish practical jokes. One day, she arrived at school to find her classmates had rigged a bucket of paint to fall on her head as she entered the classroom, ruining her brand new Easter dress. 'It's a bit of a cliché,' she shrugs. 'Comedians are always tortured souls trying to make people like them, and all that silly stuff.'

After a few weeks, the school bullies had moved on to someone else and meek and mild Jennifer quickly developed a mischievous streak. By her own admission, she was a disruptive pupil. She was always pulled up for talking in class and was more concerned with socialising than study. On a number of occasions, John and Nancy were called in to discuss their daughter's development with teachers. 'I was rowdy and I spent a lot of time in the principal's office,' says Jennifer.

With hindsight, she can link her behavioural problems directly to a difficult home life. 'I did it for attention,' she says. 'As sick as it sounds, it was the only way to get my father and my mother in the same room.' But she does have regrets about a wasted education. 'I cut off my nose to spite my face, because I was trying to get attention. I didn't take in as much as I could have. I feel quite immature. Half the time, I don't know what I'm doing. I missed out on a lot. I was a rebel and I didn't apply myself, so I have all these clichéd regrets. I'm constantly educating myself, trying to catch up.' Ironically, Jennifer was learning a skill that would provide the backbone of her future career. 'It wasn't tough to see the comedy side of me. I was a clown in school! I was not a good student and got kicked out of classes for clowning around.'

Jennifer was convinced every teacher in the school hated her. 'I think there was a "Teachers Who Hate Jennifer Aniston Anonymous" group!' One of the worst was a German teacher called Mr Piening. Jennifer recalls a particular incident involving two classroom palm trees. 'Jennifer! I want to tie a palm tree to each of your feet and throw you out the window!' he shouted, after she'd been particularly misbehaved. She also refused to take school examinations seriously. 'I doodled the answers to my SATs. I'd go a, a, b, a. Let's see, haven't had a c in a while...'

But to her parents' relief, Jennifer managed to knuckle down at the last minute. When the school eventually threatened to kick her out, she was forced to focus on her schoolwork. 'Only time I ever got As.'

While being a chatterbox didn't necessarily do her any favours in the classroom, Jennifer was never short of friends in the playground. 'I was the talker of the group and somehow I got the role of therapist among my friends. Who knows if that comes from being in a family where the parents were more like children than you were?' she shrugs. 'You kind of want to take care of everyone, which can be a bad thing, trying to be a saviour for everyone. You kind of miss out on letting them take care of you.' Jennifer's talent for counselling even led to early ambitions of becoming a psychiatrist. 'I was always the one people would drag into the locker room and say, "I've got to talk to you!"' she laughs.

Like all teenagers, Jennifer went through a teenage rebellion. At the age of 14, she started to experiment with fashion and make-up. Nancy initially imposed a 'no make-up until 16' rule but this was quickly broken. 'Jennifer has decided to copy Cleopatra!' her mother fumed.

As a child, she had practised different hairstyles on her Barbie-doll head. 'I had a big Barbie head, and I would put pink curlers in her hair and wrap the bangs around them to get the Farrah Fawcett thing down. I tried this on my own hair, too, but it never worked. You should never copy a style.'

But, as her teenage years progressed, she grew more adventurous. 'I dyed my hair a lovely purply plum colour and then orange. It was pretty bad.' Eventually, however, she settled for black. 'I had the short hair and the big black outfits and the black liquid eyeliner that made me look like a vampire, with all sorts of pins sticking out of my body parts.' When Jennifer was 14, she even attempted to pierce her own ears 'with a potato and a piece of celery'.

But it was her haircut that landed her in the most trouble. 'My parents used to scream at me because I only wore black and I had my hair cut in a modified Mohawk. My hair was shaved about an inch above the ear.' Her look would draw a number of comments, most notably from her grandmother. 'Why does she dress like a widow?' she asked John.

Aware that it would wind up her parents, Jennifer also insisted on playing music really loudly. 'I'd play it so fucking loud my mom would kick the door in.' Fitting to her fashion sense, her favourite kind of music was rock. 'I was a big fat wuss who liked Aerosmith!' she shrugs. 'I also listened to The Sex Pistols for a while, but I don't think I ever really liked them. That's one of those guilty confessions. I can't understand their music. I can't make anything out. But I thought it would help me be accepted... being the uncool fat girl!'

In the grand scheme of things, however, Jennifer describes herself as a pretty regular kid. 'I never like snuck out and slept at somebody's house. I was a pretty normal kid.' In fact, the worst she did was steal some cosmetics from a department store. 'When I was 14, my friend and I were in Webbers [a big American haberdashery] and we lifted some make-up, and that was pretty daring and bad.'

Hardly madcap behaviour, but Jennifer insists she has a few crazy antics in her closet. One memorable incident involved the pop band Duran Duran.

Having overcome her crush on Scott Baio, Jennifer moved her attentions to Simon Le Bon. 'I loved Simon. He was very cute and he had a sexy voice. I just screamed at him when I went to their concerts. My girlfriends and I had every one of their albums and every video.' Unable to watch TV at home, she would spend hours watching videos on MTV at a friend's house.

On one occasion, she set her alarm for 5am just to secure a place in line at an in-store record signing. Carrying a rose, she arrived to find there was already a queue stretching around the block. 'I waited all day and finally worked my way to fifth in line. All of a sudden, they lock the doors and everyone goes crazy. And I'm standing there with this bent rose from battling all these animals. I was bummed.'

At the height of her obsession, she even camped outside a hotel, hoping to catch a glimpse of her hero. 'I was just 12 at the time, but I look back with a blush and a giggle because it was a fun thing to do. I like being crazy and being with crazy people so long as it is always fun and nothing that really hurts.'

Looking back at the episode, Jennifer reflects on the phenomenon of fame and celebrity. 'I wonder: What did I want? What was I expecting? I don't understand it even now. I know that the real person isn't worthy of the adoration of innocent girls and yet those girls are allowed to have that, aren't they? I've been on both sides now but it doesn't make it any easier to understand.'

Alongside acting, Jennifer took up several further creative pastimes. It was a school requirement that every student learn a musical instrument. Jennifer decided to play the flute, but very soon grew tired of practising. Eventually, Nancy agreed to drop the lessons if Jennifer promised to devote more time to her studies. Art proved to be a far more favourable subject. Until this day, Jennifer continues to paint as a hobby. 'I used to paint with shading, colours and dimension, but now it's just freehand and whatever comes to mind. It was a great thing to be exposed to as a kid,' she says. One of her sketches was even exhibited at the Metropolitan Museum of Art in New York. 'I was only nine, but it was a fluke. They picked ten Steiner students to exhibit at the Met, and that was pretty cool. At the time, I was like, "So what?"'

Clearly talented, some teachers even suggested Jennifer might turn to painting professionally. Asked whether she'd consider that now, she shrugs, 'Yeah, why not? I'm sure I could if I wanted to. You can slap anything in a canvas and sell it for a ridiculous price!'

Predictably, Jennifer scored her first big break through her father, although to her disappointment it proved to be something of a false start. One day she asked Nancy, 'Mommy, do you think Daddy would let me visit the set of his new show?'

Nancy promised to make a few calls, but didn't seem to think it would be a problem. At the time, John was working on a new show called *Search For Tomorrow*. He agreed to the idea and a date was set for the visit.

When the day for Jennifer's star turn finally came, she

could hardly contain her excitement. 'I can still see this little yellow ice-skating dress that I was psyched to be in that morning. The whole experience was thrilling.'

On arrival, she was taken straight to make-up. John had pulled a few strings and managed to secure Jennifer a spot as an extra. She dutifully took up her position and obediently followed instructions from the producer. When someone came over and asked her to swap places with another girl, she thought nothing of it. Only later did she discover John had specifically requested the move. 'On the way home, Dad mentioned how I wouldn't have been picked up by the camera if our places hadn't been switched. I felt terrible, absolutely mortified and humiliated that the poor girl got bumped because of me, the daughter of the soap star. I still remember walking down Broadway in silence after he told me. I didn't have that kind of ambition. You know how there are some people who burn with this feeling of "I'm going to make it"? I never had that. But there was another thing I learned that day as an extra. In order for me to get what I'd wanted, something was compromised. What you want always comes with a price.'

In more ways than one, Jennifer had got more than she bargained for! It turned out the directors were looking for a young actress to play a runaway. Jennifer plucked up the courage to ask for an audition and to her amazement they agreed. John was blown away by his daughter's confidence. 'I'd taken her to work with me one day,' he recalls. After leaving Jennifer in a waiting room, he returned to find her on the phone plotting her first career move. 'She was on the telephone with my agent trying to sort out an audition.'

When the day of her screen test finally arrived, Jennifer was wracked with worry. She was disappointed with her performance and agonised for days afterwards, waiting for the call to come. Sadly for Jennifer, they'd offered the role to another girl. But all was not completely lost. The other actress was still waiting to hear about a movie role and hadn't yet decided whether to accept the TV part. The producers asked if Jennifer wouldn't mind coming into the studio to film the first episode. Of course, she was delighted. But further disappointment lay ahead. Just as the crew were about to start filming, they received a call to say the other actress was now available. Arriving home in floods of tears, Jennifer was distraught.

It was a painful introduction to the acting industry, but didn't discourage Jennifer in the least. One day she sat down with Nancy and announced that she wanted to enrol in drama school. A friend had introduced her to New York's High School of Performing Arts, made famous by the TV series *Fame*. 'I'd seen *Fame* I don't know how many times. I got the idea that I could go to a school for acting and get started. My dad was against it, but my mom was great in encouraging me: "Keep going, keep going."'

For a time, her admittance hung in the balance. Too late for the preliminary enrolment auditions, she had to beg for a last-minute audition. Thankfully, the school relented and allowed her to try out. She completed a four-hour audition reading two monologues: one from 'The Sign' in

Sidney Bernstein's *Window* and the other from Neil Simon's *I Ought to Be in Pictures*. The judges were impressed and offered her a place.

Jennifer fell instantly in love with her new school. She was given a black satin jacket embroidered with the school insignia. Her name was stitched in red on the left breast. She treasured the item of clothing for years. 'The school was a lot of fun. I couldn't wait to put on my tights and go in there.'

With a degree of humility, Jennifer admits she was never a star pupil. While in the junior year, she landed her first stage role in a musical. She recalls her audition song was 'Journey: Open Arms'. But approaching the performance Jennifer got cold feet and bailed. Terrified by the idea of performing in front of a large audience, she made up an excuse about an after-school job. The following year, however, she plucked up the courage to go through with a show. The production was *Turandot* and Jennifer played one of the princess' maids. 'I always got the shitty parts!' she reflects.

While her peers were focused on becoming serious actors, Jennifer was too busy enjoying herself. During rehearsals, she would often break any dramatic tension by erupting into fits of giggles. 'Any teacher there will tell you that I was the worst. I don't think they considered me to have many talents. But I didn't care. I didn't get the parts in big plays, but I definitely enjoyed myself.' One teacher in particular, 'a mean old Russian guy', told her she was a disgrace and that she should never be allowed to act in front of people. 'I wanted to make people cry, man; to move people,' she jokes. 'But I was making them laugh.'

Jennifer's 'weakness', however, would ultimately become her strength. Several tutors recognised her talent for comedy and criticism quickly turned to praise. 'My mentor, this wonderful actor teacher in the 11th grade, told me, "You've got the ability to be funny, but be careful. It can be safe and prevent you going to real places." That threw me. I never thought of myself as a comedienne.'

But Jennifer would continue to impress tutors with her breezy charm and razor-sharp comic timing. 'I sat her down and told her she would be in a sitcom,' says Anthony Abeson, a former acting teacher at the school. 'Even then she had a gift for comedy, an energy that's not easy to legislate. Some funny people are exhalers. Funny all the time; always on. They crowd people out. Jennifer was good as an inhaler as well as an exhaler. Like the tide, she always had the ability to go in and out.'

Prior to completing her course Jennifer was required to perform in an end-of-year show in front of key figures from the entertainment industry. It was the biggest project of Jennifer's life thus far, but one that wouldn't go completely to plan. At one point, it looked as if Jennifer was in line for the lead role. But her high hopes gradually diminished as she was relegated first to a supporting lead and finally to a non-speaking part. Horrified by the outcome she was convinced her acting career was over before it had even started. How would prospective agents identify her talents in an almost negligible role? Fearing humiliation, Jennifer considered skipping school the day after her performance. All the actors' names were pinned on a notice board where agents could leave contact details. To her shock, Jennifer arrived to find a number pinned beneath her name. By the end of the week, she had seven different requests.

Finally, Jennifer Aniston was on course to realising her dream. Taking Nancy's advice, she signed up freelance to three leading agents. After her graduation ceremony, Jennifer decided to spend the summer with her father in LA. Determined to set her life in order, she decided to offload the insecurities she'd carried through her teenage years. John listened patiently as she relieved herself of grievances that had weighed heavy since her parents' divorce: all the arguments, his diminished responsibilities as a father and an overall lack of emotional support throughout her childhood. Nodding with agreement at every accusation, his response was simple: he was sorry. Jennifer graciously accepted his apology. Having relinquished her anger, it was time to move on.

Chapter 4

LA Bound

Returning from her LA vacation, 18-year-old Jennifer Aniston started to plan her future career. It was the autumn of 1987 and New York's theatres were buzzing with activity. Surrounded by so much competition, Jennifer knew it wouldn't be easy to land her first professional role. Taking a deep breath, she slogged her way through countless auditions. Very soon, it became obvious she would need another source of income. Looking for a temporary cash injection, she undertook a string of menial jobs.

'I was a waitress for many years and I loved it!' she smiles. Jennifer started out at a burger joint called Jackson Hole on the Upper West Side and was 'thrilled with getting 500 bucks a week!' But Jennifer reaped more than just the financial rewards. 'I liked waiting tables. I even liked filling the damn ketchup bottles!' she insists. 'I wasn't great but I loved it. I loved the people and the food, but I was a little klutzy and forgetful... I dropped things a lot. I got orders wrong and spilled stuff on people but they were OK with it. Only one time did I have someone take my head off and yell at me!' Jennifer remembers that particular occasion well. Two foreign customers had ordered an Alpine burger ('which is just a pile of onions and mushrooms and Swiss cheese') and a Chilli burger. While carrying the food to their table, Jennifer stumbled and dropped the contents of her tray on their laps. 'They were yelling, pretty much at the top of their lungs, "You stupid... woman! You stupid... stupid..." That's all I can remember: "Stupid."'

During this period, Jennifer also reflected on her lack of application at college. While her long-term goal was to become an actress, she knew it was important to have a back-up means of professional employment. After all, she didn't want to be a waitress for the rest of her life. 'I was taking classes at night in psychology, waitressing during the day, auditioning when I could. I was like, "I've got to get out of here."' If all else failed, Jennifer reasoned she could become a shrink. 'I like to talk to people; I like people to talk to me.' In reality, she lasted just five months. 'We were into Freud and all of those guys and the different philosophies of human behaviour... and then I got a play.'

Jennifer spent the next two years religiously attending auditions. In that time, she only scored a handful of parts. 'I got a Bob's Big Boy commercial, then a part in a play.' The play was an off-Broadway production of *For Dear*

Life at the Public Theatre. 'I was pretty psyched,' recalls Jennifer. 'It was that time of your life when you don't know any better to know that you're acting in the worst play of your life.' But there was one particular performance that sticks in her mind. 'One night as I'm doing it, I realise that I'm staring straight into this huge, gaping cavern that is the mouth of Al Pacino. He's sitting in the audience next to Diane Keaton – and he's really laughing. I couldn't believe it. I made Al Pacino laugh. It was one of the greatest moments I'd ever had. A moment like that can carry you for a year or two.'

A second theatre performance soon followed in *Dancing on Checker's Grave*. As part of her role, Jennifer was required to kiss a girl on stage every night for six weeks. The plot focused on two girls who hang out in a cemetery at lunchtime talking about life and sexuality. Despite treading brand-new turf, Jennifer wasn't in the slightest bit fazed. 'I probably was thinking, wow, this is really cool, kissing a girl,' she says.

While she was certainly happy, Jennifer was by no means hitting the big time. 'I couldn't even get close to Broadway. I was always off-off-off-Broadway, but I was still happy... I'd get a job in a play, think it was great, then go right back to waitressing. Somehow, anything else seemed unattainable.' Contemplating her future, the aspiring actress wondered if she'd ever make it. Perhaps in a few years she'd simply give up and marry someone rich. 'I actually never really thought I would truly make it, considering my acting teachers were always telling me that I'm a disgrace to the theatre,' she confesses. Although she had big dreams, Jennifer was never ruthlessly ambitious. 'I was driven, but maybe I didn't have a complete enough belief in myself to give me that animal drive… I didn't have many expectations. I didn't think I was destined for greatness. I was just kind of destined for happiness.'

After two years of constant auditions, Jennifer realised it was time to plot her next move. Refusing to give up, she instead decided on a change of scenery. Having exhausted every opportunity in New York, her future lay in Los Angeles. It seemed as if every new show was being cast on the West Coast and Jennifer didn't want to miss out. Besides, her father had offered her a place to stay until she could find an apartment of her own.

In the summer of 1989, Jennifer took a plane to LA and set up several meetings. She describes her experience as 'the scariest thing'. People would constantly ask about the work she'd done in New York. 'I hadn't done much, so everything on my resume was made up.'

A change of address didn't necessarily guarantee the success Jennifer desired and once again she was forced to seek out part-time employment. Her first job was as a telemarketer selling time-shares in the Poconos. She lasted just two weeks. 'I was so bad,' she says. 'I never could have been worse at something. I didn't sell one. I just sat there and doodled. They actually scheduled your work at the worst time, around the time when people are sitting down to dinner. The guy sitting next to me kept selling time-share after time-share, and I thought, Well, you must be an irritating person who somehow managed to get these people on the phone. I was immediately apologetic:

"Oh, I'm so sorry!" I just felt terrible I didn't like disturbing people.' But she admits the universally hated profession was good practice for showbusiness. 'You have to have a thick skin!'

After her short stint in telesales, Jennifer tried her hand as a bike courier. This time she managed to stick it out for three months. 'I wasn't the most coordinated on the bike with the cars and everything. But I loved it. I had fun. I was on a bike and I looked like one of those cool guys. The problem was, I just didn't do it very well and eventually I got fired.' A succession of jobs followed, including work at an advertising agency and as a receptionist in a skincare centre.

Fortunately, it wasn't long before she landed her first part in the rather unfortunate TV movie *Camp Cucamonga*, tagged 'the zaniest, most hilarious summer vacation ever!' Set in a summer camp for teenagers, the plotline revolved around the camp's owner believing a local handyman was in fact a camp inspector preparing to shut the place down. It was universally panned.

Next up was a role in a TV series called *Molloy*. Her co-star was a young comic actress called Mayim Bialik, better known as the central character in popular sitcom *Blossom*. The pair enjoyed a great on-screen chemistry, but sadly the series was cancelled mid-season.

While the roles did little for Jennifer's acting credibility, they undoubtedly boosted her bank balance. With greater funds in the bank, she could afford to move out of her father's house and into a place of her own. She chose a place in the trendy Laurel Canyon area of Hollywood, known as The Hill. But the image was far more glamorous than the reality. Jennifer's flat was a low-rent communal housing project. 'Whenever the inspector came round, we had to pull out our stoves and hide them.'

Her social network included a group of aspiring actors, writers, directors and production executives, who all lived on the same street. 'We were called the Hill People,' smiles Jennifer. 'We always hung out together, and we were very incestuous, very concerned about each other. Everyone was involved in everyone else's life.'

To this day, Jennifer remains close to several members of the group. Unlike so many other star-struck actors, Jennifer refused to ditch her original friends in favour of a glamorous Hollywood set. 'I think the wonderful thing about Jen is that she didn't become well known and then suddenly adopt another lot of friends who are fabulous,' says her best friend Kristin Hahn. 'She's kept the things she's had since she was 19.'

Kristin goes on to describe their first meeting. 'I had a little apartment about the size of a bathroom and one night Jen came hopping down my stairs. I was taking something out of the oven, I turned round and there she was. She had that sweet glow about her. She just oozed love and she still does. We became instantly crazy about each other and spent every day together for the next few years.' One of the few lucky enough to have a steady income, Kristin worked as a producer's assistant on the TV show *Cheers*. 'Jen would come and hang out with me during the day, lie on my couch, and talk about how she was never going to work.'

The 'Hill People' provided Jennifer with an essential

support network. They would regularly meet up every Sunday for a barbecue and share mutual complaints about the industry and fears for the future. Over time, the intimate group gradually grew larger. 'Everybody just kept moving up there,' exclaims Jennifer. 'In all these houses were all our friends. And everybody watched out for everybody. We never left the hill.'

On the occasions they did step outside of their safe haven, it was usually on an organised road trip. 'Eight of us shacked up in one hotel room in Santa Barbara for three days,' laughs Kristin. 'Our friend Michael Sanville, a photographer, would always come up with ideas for crazy shoots, mostly based around some ploy to get us naked.'

It was obvious Jennifer and her friends shared a unique camaraderie. On her 22nd birthday, Jennifer arrived home to find the apartment plastered with pictures of her crush. 'They covered every surface – even the fridge!' she says, shaking her head. 'It was so silly and embarrassing.'

Although the Hill People were a mixed-gender group, a strong bond developed between female members and the clan would often head out on 'women only' nights. 'The rule was that you were not allowed to talk to men; it was all about women worshipping each other – dancing, drinking and having a blast,' says Kristin.

Jennifer also initiated a 'women's circle'. Armed with candles and personal mementoes, women would meet in the woods, sit down in a circle, hold hands and talk. 'There's such catty bullshit that goes on,' complains Jennifer. 'Women have to become nicer to each other... My girlfriends and I just started this circle. I remember the first time we did it – this one girl was silent through the whole thing and then at the end she was just weeping. She had this huge enlightening kind of experience being with these women. Women are awesome, especially together as a group, so kind and warm and wonderful.'

With a little help from her friends, Jennifer was clearly blossoming. 'That was a great time for her,' says her half-brother Johnny. 'You could tell something was happening, that she was spreading her wings.'

Her professional life, meanwhile, was ticking along nicely. Following *Molloy*, she scored a role in the TV adaptation of hit teen flick *Ferris Bueller's Day Off*. Jennifer was cast as Ferris's little sister Jeanie, played by Jennifer Grey in the original movie. Everyone was certain the show would be a success, but after just 13 episodes it was consigned to the scrapheap and once again Jennifer was out of work.

A handful of forgettable performances followed, including a spot on comedy sketch show *The Edge* and a guest slot on the wildly experimental sitcom *Herman's Head*. Jennifer explains the concept: 'It's a guy's head, and inside of it are all the little people who are the brain – making decisions – and you saw them inside of his head. It sounds crazy, but it was actually really fun.'

Unable to turn down work, Jennifer found herself trapped in a world of failing sitcoms. 'I was the sitcom graveyard queen,' she laments. 'Early on in my career I didn't do myself any favours. I made poor choices. I didn't know where I was going.' Actress Andrea Bendewald, a friend since high school, agrees. 'She spent five years working on shows that weren't great, but she learned how to stay in there. It made her a veteran.'

Too scared to set her standards any higher, Jennifer embraced a world of failing TV shows. 'Back then it was familiar and safe, and now you have no idea what's around the corner,' she reasons. Convinced by her agent that she would only ever find fame on the small screen, Jennifer was petrified of auditioning for movie roles. 'I hated him for that, because I thought, You have no faith in me.' His lack of confidence evoked uncomfortable childhood memories. 'It's like your father, who instilled doubts in you as a kid.'

After much deliberation, she plucked up enough courage to read for the silver screen. But, following a precedent already set with her TV career, her choice of script was often poor. Her big screen debut came in 1993 with the low-budget horror flick *Leprechaun*, starring 3ft 6in actor Warwick Davis, whose past accolades included Wicket the Ewok in *Return of the Jedi*. The plot revolved around a leprechaun who sets out on a murderous rampage. Taking the female lead, Jennifer played a young teen determined to kill the evil midget with a four-leaf clover.

It was a ridiculous premise. Jennifer knew the film would be corny, but the director convinced her it was great comedy. Despite a meagre $1 million budget, the film made a massive profit grossing more than eight times that amount at the US box office. Considered a success, it spawned a mammoth five sequels. Surprisingly, none of them would feature Jennifer Aniston. On attending the final screening, she snuck out before the end. 'I was horrified,' she says, 'and not in the wonderful way that *Scream* horrifies you.' Even today, Jennifer has trouble talking about the experience. 'I've denied this movie for years,' she screeches. 'I deny that movie. I deny it was me in it. My apologies to Mark Jones who directed it, but I deny it, I deny it, I deny it!

'I still have a scar from that fucking movie, can you believe that?' she says, pointing to the cruel reminder. The offending mark can be found on the back of her left hand, between her thumb and forefinger. The accident occurred during a scene where Jennifer was required to poke the leprechaun in the eye with a billy club as it tried to attack her in a police car. She scratched her hand on the door lock while trying to wrestle free.

By now, Jennifer was beginning to question her career choices. *Leprechaun* proved to be one duff movie choice too many and she decided it was time to reconfigure her game plan. Since she was a child, Jennifer had always been conscious of her looks. Having her photo taken was a traumatic experience and something she always tried to avoid. 'On family trips, Mom would go, "OK, get in together! We'll take a picture." And I would just be horrified. I felt really uncomfortable,' she shudders. It's a phobia she still suffers from today. Despite being one of the world's most fanciable females, she continues to shy away from the camera. 'It's a hang-up I have. I become extremely embarrassed because there are people walking by and you're there having your photo taken.'

But even in the comfort of her own home, Jennifer has never been happy with her appearance. 'I have a kind of love-hate relationship with the mirror at home. With the way you look and perceive how you look, there are good days and there are bad days. Some days are better.'

Unknowingly, her mum would continually put pressure on Jennifer to look good. 'My mom was a model and an actress, and she knew what was beautiful... I don't want to paint a shallow picture of my mother, but how you looked was so important... She was very focused on beauty, but I didn't care about it as much. She would say, "Put your face on" and I would believe her. That's where the seed gets planted... Your mother is going, "Your eyes are too close together, so when you put your eyeliner on you have to draw the lines up here. Like this, because your eyes are already too small. And your face is too wide and, see, honey, you have your father's mouth so you're going to have to draw lines around it." You got to the point where you felt like you were the ugliest duckling on the planet.'

During her teenage years, she would use make-up as a mask to hide behind. It was only when a boyfriend diplomatically suggested she try wearing less that she actually toned it down. 'I was an unfortunate-looking teenager. I never felt beautiful, ever. I guess that's why I had to be funny... The make-up I'd wear was unbelievable. Then one of my first boyfriends in California said, "You are so much more beautiful to me without make-up," and I couldn't believe it. Finally, I stopped wearing it.' Once Jennifer had packed up her powder palette and consigned her overflowing make-up bag to the back of the bathroom shelf, she was overcome by a wave of liberation. 'I didn't care. This is me, who I am. I don't know what I was trying to prove, what I was hiding, with all that stuff on my face.'

Regardless of her own personal hang-ups, Jennifer never once considered body image might restrict her career options. But, thus far, she had never encountered the cruel reality of Hollywood head on. One day a casting director asked Jennifer to turn up to the audition in a leotard and tights. Weighing in at 130 lb, Jennifer jokingly turned to her agent and said, "Well, this should blow it for me!"

To her shock and amazement, her agent was nodding in agreement. 'Actually, I've been meaning to talk to you about that...'

For the next ten minutes, Jennifer had her body discussed like a defunct piece of machinery. She was out of shape and subsequently out of work. 'I was horrified. I was convinced I had a good body. My mom always told me I was kind of round.' After the initial shock, Jennifer came to value her agent's advice. 'My agent gave it to me straight,' she says. 'It was the nicest thing he ever did. I wasn't getting lots of jobs 'cause I was too heavy. That's the disgusting thing about Hollywood. I didn't even know I was overweight until someone told me. I hate it that your self worth is metered by how much you weigh.'

In reality, Jennifer was never fat. 'I was just Greek,' she protests, 'and Greeks are round, with big asses and big boobs. My dad used to say I had a behind you could serve tea off.' Much later in her career she would joke, 'I hear that British men love that old Venus figure, that's what a woman should be – voluptuous. Maybe I should move to London.'

While the stunned actress graciously accepted her agent's criticisms, she still curses that day 'because, from then on, I became body conscious'. It was something she'd never experienced before. As a teenager, she had successfully steered clear of the skinny syndrome. Instead, she wore clothes to complement her fuller figure. 'I never wore jeans, only huge sweaters and big skirts because I was hippy.'

Although Jennifer protests she never had a weight problem, she concedes her eating habits were unhealthy. 'I ate everything that was bad for me.' Often out of work, she would sit around watching TV and snacking from the fridge. 'I ate too many mayonnaise sandwiches,' she sighs. 'Mayonnaise on white bread is the most delicious thing in the world. My favourite was tuna-mayo, but with the tuna left out.'

Determined to sort her diet out, she visited a nutritionist. 'She nearly threw me out of her office,' laughs Jennifer. Over the next few months, she gave up snacking on white bread and mayonnaise, ditched fried food and cut down on burgers. Rather than adopt a script diet regime, she opted for the Nutri System, an eating plan she would later publicly recommend on *The Howard Stern Show*. 'It's not a diet, it's a way of life. It got to the point where I was so sick of gimmicks: "Oh, this week, I'll have oil on the side, no butter – no fun." Like most women, I was fed up with having to look like something I wasn't. It was too painful, not to mention a pain in the ass. I started to eat healthy and work out. I mean – I had never done anything.'

An advocate of healthy eating and regular exercise, she

criticises the multitude of 'weird' diets on the market. 'There are so many awful fads that you can go through and it's not worth it. It's just not where your mind should be focused. You should just focus on being content and, if you want to exercise, do it because you know it gives you satisfaction. And eat healthily for the same reason.'

Thanks to her efforts, Jennifer lost 20lb in the space of 12 months. 'It was amazing to see this thing emerge,' she says, looking at her chest. 'I never knew I had this body in me... I went through the baby-fat period and then that kind of shaved off. It's a common thing for people to go through but it all works out in the end.' Today she is an advocate of the Zone Diet, an eating plan based on balancing protein and carbohydrate levels rather than calorific content. 'It was the only thing that made sense. How are you supposed to live on grapefruit? Please.' But she still takes time to indulge in her favourite high-calorie treats, such as bacon cheeseburgers with extra crispy fries. 'I'll send them back if they're not crispy enough!' She also has a habit of scooping the insides out of bagels. 'But that's not strange,' she shrugs.

As much as Jennifer hates the unrealistic ideals Hollywood inflicts upon young women, she admits it's an unavoidable obstacle in her line of work. 'It's scary,' she observes, 'how Hollywood treats you like this completely different person when you're thin.' Even her father John describes Tinsel Town as 'an equal opportunities deflater'.

'TV is definitely guilty of putting out unrealistic images of what is socially acceptable. I'm guilty of it, too,' she admits. 'The beauty magazines in particular are there to feed on women's low self-esteem. They'll make fun of you if you're too fat and then tear you down if you're too thin. You just can't win. I am so thankful for this life but I don't feel beautiful all the time. The majority of the time I don't.'

Weight loss undoubtedly changed the course of Jennifer Aniston's career path, but she adamantly refutes it was ever the key to a happier life. 'I was just as happy before I was thinner,' she insists. 'My life wasn't different, except people, mostly men, changed.'

It was never Jennifer's intention to be a sex symbol. From day one, she simply wanted to act. 'I didn't want my looks to be my only ticket, because I didn't feel I had that one to ride on. What I do is not about looking good,' she says defiantly. 'People who want to look good all the time, they're a different kind of actor.' But her weight loss obviously had an impact and she started to land more roles. 'I started getting hired, which made me realise "so that's what this is about".'

Aside from an obscure series entitled *Sunday Funnies*, her next big project was the sitcom *Muddling Through*. Starring stand-up comedian Stephanie Hodge, the show centred around a white-trash motel owner recently released from prison after shooting her cheating husband. Jennifer would play the eldest daughter left in charge of the motel. It seemed an ideal opportunity to showcase her comedic skills. But, in another turn of bad luck, the show was shelved indefinitely (episodes were later shown in July 1994). Although this was familiar territory for Jennifer, hiding her disappointment still proved tough. Speaking about her early failed forays into television, she said, 'They've all gotten on the air except one, but they last maybe six episodes and then they are never heard of. And you think that's sort of sad. But there's a reason for it.'

As Jennifer quite rightly predicted, fate was working its magic behind the scenes. While network bosses deliberated over *Muddling Through*, Jennifer was invited to audition for another sitcom called *Friends Like These*. At the time, she had no idea of how successful the show would be. But her luck was about to change. Later shortened to *Friends*, this particular sitcom would last the distance. Jennifer Aniston's ticket to international superstardom had finally arrived.

Chapter 5

Making New Friends

After years of waiting for her big break, when it eventually came, Jennifer's life spun into overdrive. Almost overnight, she was cast in a role that would ultimately make her a household name. The brainchild of three producers who met while studying at Brandeis University in Massachusetts, *Friends* was based around a group of 20-somethings living in New York. Rather than focusing on any one lead, the show would rely on an ensemble effort. There would be six characters in total: Monica (a chef with an obsession for tidiness), Ross (her neurotic older brother, whose pregnant wife left him for another woman), Chandler (a wisecrack), Joey (a dim-witted actor), Phoebe (a masseuse/folk singer) and Rachel (Monica's spoiled high-school pal).

Initially, Jennifer's agent had suggested she read for the role of Monica. But, when it came to casting, another young actress, Courteney Cox, had her eye firmly on the part. Jennifer was ambivalent and slowly found herself drawn towards the character of Rachel. Having ditched her fiancé at the altar in favour of a life less ordinary, Rachel turned up on Monica's doorstep in a damp wedding dress. Having decided to stick around, she would take up a job at the local coffee shop Central Perk. 'I was torn between reading for Rachel and Monica,' she says. 'But Rachel felt right. I'm so much more Rachel... More neurotic than Monica, a bit more offbeat.'

The producers obviously agreed. Two hours after her audition, they called up and offered Jennifer the job. 'It happened so fast,' she exclaims. 'I went in, read the script, laughed out loud, got home and an hour later had the part. It was a done deal and I was beyond thrilled!'

Executive producer Kevin Bright was instantly impressed. Without a shadow of a doubt, he'd found his Rachel Green. 'She was the part,' he says. 'She was funny. She was pretty. It all came through in one big stroke.'

Jennifer had fallen in love with the part, but at the time she was still committed to the TV show *Muddling Through*. 'I had two other jobs and they weren't going to let me go to do *Friends*,' she recalls. 'I remember doing a photo shoot with the cast and having to stand out of some photos just in case this other show got picked up.'

While the future of *Muddling Through* was uncertain, Jennifer was already convinced she wanted to work on *Friends*. In an attempt to wrangle free of her contract, she met up with the producer and begged him to let her free. 'I remember having a girlfriend call me and say, "I'm auditioning for your part on *Friends* because I heard you're getting replaced. Could you help me with the audition?" And I was, like, "God! No! Not yet. Let's just wait till all the nails are in the coffin.'"

Fortunately, fate intervened, *Muddling Through* was shelved and Jennifer was able to accept the part.

Eventually, the producers cast all six roles, but the search for perfect candidates wasn't easy. Producer David Crane called it 'a long and hard affair… It wasn't as if we saw eight guys who could play Chandler or six girls who were right for Phoebe, and picked the best one.'

They already had David Schwimmer in mind for the part of Ross. Aside from a few features, he'd appeared briefly in *NYPD* and *The Wonder Years*. Matthew Perry, who had played opposite River Phoenix in *A Night In The Life of Jimmy Reardon*, was 'the only person who made Chandler Bing come alive', while Lisa Kudrow (a guest star on the sitcom *Mad About You*) shaped up to be the perfect Phoebe. The role of Joey was also given to a relative unknown, Matt LeBlanc. In fact, the only star with any meaty roles already under her belt was Courteney Cox. The former teen model had appeared in two Bruce Springsteen videos, the movie *Ace Ventura: Pet Detective* and as Michael J Fox's girlfriend in *Family Ties*.

While no one could predict quite how successful *Friends* would be, Jennifer had a good feeling about the show. 'It's all about relationships,' she told journalists. 'And people really need to see something that they can relate to – real-life situations.' After reading the script, she quickly realised this was more than just a run-of-the-mill slapdash sitcom. 'A lot of the TV shows I did before were "ba-de-bing, ba-de-boom" comedy and weren't real. I love comedy when it comes from the truth of a situation. That's what I love about *Friends*. As funny as it is, they work really hard not to make it cheesy and jokey – it's based on reality.'

Still, given past performances, she was reluctant to pin her hopes on any longevity. As she would herself admit, 'I'd done about seven hundred failed shows before *Friends*, and there was no reason to believe that this would be any different.'

The pilot show was shot in the summer of 1994 in the Warner Brothers studios. Immediately after the cast wrapped, the producers asked them to hang back and record the now infamous opening sequence of *Friends*, which involved the gang dancing in a heated fountain. Originally, the sequence was intended to play out under the credits but network executives felt it was too cliquey and 'locked the viewer out'. Eventually, the producers compromised by editing in shots from throughout the series.

By now, the cast had already bonded. Aside from Matthew Perry and Jennifer, none of the actors was previously acquainted. Matthew was a friend of fellow Hill girl Kristin Hahn. 'We were drinking buddies from nights downing shots in dodgy Hollywood sake joints,' smiles Matthew.

One day, Kristin invited her new pal back to the Hill house 'and our dog at the time, named Brad, bit him on the ass as he was going upstairs,' she giggles. Jennifer and

Matthew kept in touch and were already buddies by the time they started filming *Friends*. 'She's the worst driver in the history of drivers!' he joked to the remaining co-stars. 'If I know she's going somewhere, I stay home.'

Jennifer would frown, mockingly protesting her innocence. 'I'm just late... Well, we're all late sometimes. I'm a very fast driver, and I just think I can get places faster than I do.'

Even after filming the first show, the producers knew they had a hit on their hands. The NBC TV network agreed and gave the green light for an entire series. As a thank-you gesture, the director Jimmy Burrows flew the cast to Las Vegas for an all-expenses-paid jolly. But it was also an opportunity to savour their last moments of anonymity. Jennifer has fond memories of the trip. 'Papa [a nickname Jennifer gave to Jimmy] took us out to dinner and said, "You don't know what you're about to embark on. You better take care of each other." We had no idea what he was talking about. Then he gave us each $500 and said, "Enjoy it. This is the last time you'll be able to walk through a casino without being bothered." Papa is one psychic Jew!'

The first episode of *Friends* aired on US TV screens on 22 September 1994 (British viewers had to wait an extra six months). The show was an instant hit with viewers and a *Friends* frenzy swept the nation. 'It's a dreamboat ride,' said one NBC executive of the show. 'A bona fide hit.'

Suddenly the six unknown actors were household names.

'That first year, we shot to number one in summer re-runs,' says Jennifer, still with a degree of disbelief. 'The six of us at *Friends* would be saying to each other: "You all right? You OK? Jeez! This is intense!"'

Audiences instantly identified with the characters and quickly picked out their favourites. Jennifer's character Rachel was particularly popular. Her flustered hand gestures and quirky facial expressions quickly enamoured. But it was Jennifer's impeccable comic timing that proved to be a real ratings winner. At last, her misguided 'classroom clown' talents had finally found a purpose. Asked how she got into 'Rachel mode', Jennifer would shrug, 'You think of every rich Connecticut girl you ever came across.'

Her production team, however, were less dismissive of Jennifer's acting skills. 'Jennifer is wonderful at playing zany – she's always pushing to do more physical comedy. But she can also break your heart,' praised *Friends* co-creater David Crane.

Her co-stars were equally complimentary. 'To me, Jennifer has a real artist's heart. Jennifer is all love and emotion,' Lisa Kudrow told reporters. 'Acting is the perfect occupation for a person like that. It seems to me she just came into the world like that. Like some people have blue eyes or long legs – it's a personality trait you can't do anything about.'

Giving her own assessment of the Rachel phenomenon, Courteney Cox added, 'She's a real girl's girl. Guys love her, but women really love her and are not threatened by her. It's a really good sign when someone has a lot of good girlfriends.'

But it wasn't just the girls Jennifer had won over. A self-fashioned funnyman himself, Matt LeBlanc was suitably impressed by the side-splitting star. 'Jen doesn't like to overwork things,' says Matt. 'She has a real fresh loose-cannony thing about her that's real exciting to work with.'

Jennifer would also develop a very close on-screen relationship with her co-star David Schwimmer. The Ross 'n' Rachel storyline kept viewers gripped throughout the first season, if not the whole lifespan of the show. The script dictated Ross had always harboured secret feelings for his sister's school pal Rachel. When she opted to move in with Monica, these passions were inevitably reignited. At the end of the first series, Rachel dashes to meet Ross at the airport after discovering his true feelings for her. By a cruel twist of fate, however, Ross has embarked on an affair with an old work colleague while on a business trip. This was just the beginning of a rollercoaster relationship that would become a household obsession.

One website even claimed Jennifer and David Schwimmer were lovers in real life. 'Someone was saying how they'd seen us kissing in a mall,' laughed Jennifer. 'I certainly didn't know about it and I don't think he did either – although we'd probably have enjoyed it, had it happened, ha ha ha! But, you know, I'm rumoured to be having sex with every famous man in Hollywood; and the truth is I haven't had sex with anyone famous.'

More than ever before, Jennifer felt at home on the set of *Friends*. All those past years of emotional turbulence, financial instability and creative doubt could finally be forgotten. Every day she would drive into the Warner Brothers lot, excited about the day ahead. But her journey wasn't always quite so stress-free. One morning, while pulling into the studio driveway, Jennifer accidentally cut somebody off. An angry driver screeched to a halt behind her and, bounding from his vehicle, bombarded the shocked actress with a barrage of angry words. As it turned out, the furious driver was a big-wig director, but at the time Jennifer didn't recognise him. He also failed to recognise the station's latest darling. 'He just proceeded to scream at me at the top of his lungs every profanity you can imagine,' she says. 'He would not stop: "What the fuck is your problem? Who the hell do you think you are? You shouldn't be allowed in a car! You shouldn't be allowed on the road! You shouldn't be allowed. I don't know who you are, but I'm going to find out and make your life miserable!" The only word that came out of my mouth, the only word I could think of at the time was "Why?" And he said, "Because you're a fucking terrible driver and you shouldn't be allowed to drive."'

After he'd gone, Jennifer turned to a security guard for back up. 'What's his problem?' she fumed.

The guard proceeded to tell Jennifer that she'd been arguing with one of the biggest names in television. 'You might want to send him some flowers,' he politely suggested.

'Are you kidding?' snorted Jennifer. 'No fucking way I'm sending that man flowers.'

Subsequently, the director put a name to his 'driver from hell'. Three hours later, a large bouquet of flowers arrived on the *Friends* set. This was just one small indication of the power and respect Jennifer Aniston was amassing.

Thankfully, life on set was far more amicable! In fact, Jennifer couldn't have hoped for a better dream-team of co-workers. TV critics would frequently comment that the root of the *Friends* success story lay in the genuine chemistry shared between the on-screen stars. These were more than just a group of friends who smiled for the camera. While the cameras would stop rolling come the end of the day, the jokes never did. It was all too obvious a cliché, but the *Friends* cast really were becoming best mates. 'We all clicked within days of shooting the pilot,' smiles Jennifer.

Lisa Kudrow agrees, 'There's nothing like the group of us on the show,' she enthuses. 'There is a bond between us, maybe like between people who have been in war. We've been through so much together that no one else can understand.' She pauses. 'I mean war in a good way.'

Jennifer developed a strong relationship with each of her co-stars and cherished them all for very different reasons. 'The boys are like brothers,' she cooed. 'Especially Matt LeBlanc. He's the guy who says, "Hey, they mess with you, tell me about it and I'll take care of them." When I first met him, I was scared of him, but he's the biggest teddy bear on the planet!' She shared a similarly tender relationship with on-screen lover David Schwimmer, referring to him as a 'goombah'. All joking aside, she was also in awe of his professionalism. 'David Schwimmer is the most committed, talented person. We watch out for each other in our scenes, and David's got that director's eye. He can fix scenes.' Her long-running friendship with Matthew Perry, meanwhile, had become something of a family tie. 'I've gotten so mad at Matthew – we've all gotten so mad at each other – but we can do that because we love each other that much. We have this wonderful bond where I feel protected, loved and cared about – and it's not bullshit.'

In spite of her good looks, Jennifer proved to be much more than a man hook. As Courteney Cox had quite astutely pointed out, she also had a great relationship with women. Unlike so many other TV shows, there was never any bitchiness or female rivalry on set. 'The girls are very close and always will be,' said Jennifer proudly. 'Try getting us out of our dressing rooms when one of us is needing to talk – it's impossible. Our poor [assistant directors] are saying, 'We need you downstairs.' And we're like, "This is priority. Friend in need!" Courteney Cox is the doer, the organiser; I'm the emotional one; and Lisa's the intellectual, very cerebral.'

Over time, the girls would become extremely close friends. Jennifer and Courteney were almost inseparable and Jennifer would later become godmother to Courteney's child.

Jennifer recalls the day they first met. 'I remember meeting Courteney and I was enraptured. First of all, that someone's face could be that beautiful. And it goes way beyond that. Her spirit is infectious. She's somebody you are around and you just want to be a better person. You want to live! She lives so fully. She and David Arquette [Courteney's husband] are something to witness. They have no inhibitions, they are very forthcoming, and that's just a different road to take, where everything is worn out on her sleeve. She's inside out. She's like a hairless cat.'

While on set, Jennifer earned herself a reputation for being the messiest of the bunch. One taken-aback journalist described her trailer as 'a hotel suite that's received a polite trashing'. Empty packets of cigarettes littered the coffee table, while clothes and screwed-up tissues littered the floor. In the corner of the room stood a vase of very sorry-looking wilted flowers. As if on cue Matthew Perry barged into the room, plucked a cloth bag from the sofa and held it aloft saying, with feigned disgust, 'Is this one-half of your bra?' The journalist didn't know where to look. Jennifer simply giggled.

By contrast, Jennifer's best mate Courteney was fastidiously tidy – just like her alter ego Monica. 'Courteney's a neat freak. And thank God, because my dressing room would be a mess if it wasn't for her,' laughed Jennifer.

But, while Courteney could take the moral high ground when it came to organisational skills, both girls were equally poor at time keeping. Every morning Jennifer would ring Courteney during her 20-minute drive to work, just to check how late she would be.

The girls would often spend hours gossiping in their trailers, swapping clothes and beauty techniques. 'I love plucking my eyebrows,' laughs Jennifer. 'It's like my Zen time. I get that magnifying mirror and I go to town.' Often Jennifer would ask Courteney to do the honours. 'Courteney is the only one I ever let pluck. She did it once and I pluck hers… But she lets me pluck hers more.' The girls would also stand in front of the mirror and compare emerging signs of cellulite – something that's hard to fathom, given that collectively they probably weighed less than one regular human being. 'Oh yeah! Me and Courteney and Lisa do it to each other constantly,' Jennifer would confess. 'Look at that, look at that! And then we make each other look at it. It's the most bizarre thing!'

Very soon, the friends were able to support each other in more than just a professional capacity. If anyone had a problem in their personal life, the others would be on hand to offer advice. On numerous occasions, the girls would keep cast and crew waiting while they discussed matters of 'life or death' importance. Whenever Jennifer was down, she always found comfort in Lisa's soothing laughter. 'No matter what problem any of us had, there was always Lisa Kudrow's laugh. She has one of the all-time greats, like a rollercoaster going up – tick, tick, tick – before the big drop. There she goes! Then she can't speak. She cries. And we all lose it and can't do any shooting for two hours. What's that saying? Friends are the family we choose.'

Lisa was equally complimentary about Jennifer. 'Jennifer is all about love. Whatever you're doing, whatever you're wearing, she loves it. If you hate your dress, she'll say, "But, wow, look at your hair!" She's good through and through, and that comes out.'

'We're all really close,' Courteney would boast. 'The girls are probably my two best friends in the world. There's unconditional love between us which means we always sort out any problems between us.' Attempting to quantify the bond between herself and Courteney,

Jennifer told one reporter, 'Let's put it this way... if we were lesbians, we would marry each other.'

Unbelievably, the girls never grew sick of each other's company. Every lunchtime they would all head down to the studio commissary together. A creature of habit, Jennifer would always order the same dish. 'Every single day she eats a salad and she orders it the exact same way,' Courteney would laugh, amused by her friend's clockwork predictability. 'Light on garbanzo beans, turkey and some kind of lemon dressing made by a wonderful craft-services woman we call Mama, and pecorino cheese – Jennifer's favourite.'

Occasionally, the girls would venture further afield on their breaks. 'When it's lunchtime and someone wants to eat off set, it's understood there's an open invitation to lunch for whoever wants to go,' said Lisa Kudrow. 'But a lot of the time us girls all go to the same place together.'

Although the women naturally gravitated towards each other, there was never a male/female divide on set. 'We're all good friends!' Lisa told one journalist.

'The guys often eat together too, or they'll want to play video games in their room or something,' added Courteney.

At that moment, Matthew Perry interrupted. 'But don't you love us guys, too? We thought we were tight with you girls!'

Pretending to act flustered, Courteney screeched, 'I said all six of us were close!'

'No you didn't!' blustered Matthew.

'But I meant it, though! We're all so close we can take hot baths together!' replied Courteney on cue.

'Yes, but first we walk upstairs to our dressing rooms and work things out!' smiled Matthew.

These sort of playful exchanges became commonplace between the cast members. 'They're, well, OK!' joked Lisa, when asked to give her opinion on the boys. 'No, we all like each other and once in a while we'll be waiting around the set for something and we'll just gather in someone's room to hang out until things get going on the shoot. The guys do tend to hang out with the guys and the girls with the girls, but maybe we've been conditioned to behave like that – everywhere we go we're introduced in alphabetical order and that immediately puts us ladies first!'

All jokes aside, the pals would frequently seek invaluable advice from members of the opposite sex. Matt LeBlanc admitted that he would always turn to Jennifer and Lisa for advice and that all-important female perspective. 'Jen is just an angel with great advice all the time and Lisa is really, really smart and creative,' he cooed. 'Courteney is like a big sister.'

Matthew Perry, meanwhile, preferred to turn to his male pals for help. 'It depends on the kind of problem. I'd feel comfortable going to anyone. David has a very strong business head and he's very creative. Matty is really smart about relationships and how to handle sticky situations with people.'

This last comment proved to be a point of disagreement. 'I can only sort out other people's relationships, though!' Matt scoffed.

Often, the girls would indulge their inquisitive male co-stars with stories of sex and intimacy. 'They love it,' giggled Jennifer. 'All boys do. We've gotten into some pretty intense conversations about sex and it's such a kick for us because they love hearing it, and we really go off on it sometimes just to entertain them really!'

To outsiders, such talk of camaraderie may have sounded clichéd, but the off-screen relationship between the actors was undeniably sincere. 'Upstairs is just kind of a less funny version of the show that goes on downstairs,' joked Matthew.

While no day on set was ever the same, Jennifer enjoyed the routine of working with the same friendly faces. An average work day would involve an initial run-through of scripts in the famous fake Manhattan living room. Slowly stepping through each scene, the actors would plot every move and quickly commit them to memory. The director would then draft in a 'second team' of stand-ins who would move through the same steps, while the director decided where to position the cameras. During breaks in rehearsal, the cast would fawn all over each other. It was not uncommon to find Matt running his fingers through Jennifer's hair or Courteney perched comfortably on Matthew's lap. Of course, their relationships were completely platonic, but as one crew member quite rightly pointed out, 'If you worked on a show with girls like this, wouldn't you do lots of touching, too?'

'What's with all the touching?' enquired one onlooker.

'What can I say?' shrugged Jennifer. 'We just love each other.'

'In another profession, you might all be brought up on charges,' he laughed.

'Well,' she said, smiling, 'it's almost come to that with Matthew Perry.'

Finally, it seemed as if Jennifer had found her spiritual home. 'I just love it here,' she would enthuse to friends. 'This is something better than work!' In fact, her only complaint was that she couldn't swear on the show. 'I wish we could ad-lib "fuck" into our TV show. I love that word. Maybe only my character, Rachel, should be allowed to say it though. I wish we could be like *Absolutely Fabulous* and swear and talk about sex and drugs. That would be great!'

Sadly, the NBC TV network didn't quite agree! But it was a small price to pay for being part of a show that would ultimately become one of America's most popular sitcoms ever.

The first series of *Friends* ended with great reviews and even better viewing figures. The show was officially a success and each of the actors went home happy with a pay packet of $35,000 an episode. Jennifer was in shock. A bonus this big was certainly an improvement on the dollar tips she'd stashed away as a waitress. But little did she know, this was just a taste of things to come. Compared to the massive fortune awaiting Jennifer, this was just a drop in the ocean.

Chapter 6

Rachel Mania

While the success of *Friends* was undeniably an ensemble effort, Jennifer Aniston increasingly became the focus of attention. Only it wasn't just her acting skills people were interested in. Women all over the globe were fascinated by her hairstyle. By the end of the first series, Jennifer's hair had taken on an identity of its own and become an unofficial seventh cast member. Initially known as the 'shag' and later the 'Rachel', Jennifer's wispy razor-cut hairstyle, which curved around her face in an oval, was actually a happy accident. 'My friend Chris took a razor blade and just chopped,' she explains. At the time she thought nothing of the cut and was totally unprepared for the furore that ensued. 'It was such a surprise,' she admits. 'I always thought I'd seen the style before... I guess I don't spend too much time trying to figure it out anyway.'

What was essentially an emergency measure instantly became the most coveted hairstyle in TV history. Hairdressers would grow sick and tired of requests for 'the Rachel'. Even public figures like Hillary Clinton and Cherie Booth revamped their image with the cut. Jennifer was quite bemused by the whole phenomenon. As a child, she'd always been ridiculed for her bizarre haircuts. Now they were a source of envy. 'The hair thing is pretty ironic, because I've always hated my hair,' she shrugged. 'It's always been curly and I've wanted it to be straight all my life. I had bad hair days with the humidity. People like my hair so much? Take it!'

Her co-star Lisa Kudrow was far more complimentary about the cut. 'It's a great haircut,' said Kudrow. 'But most women just don't wear it as well as Jennifer. They can cut it however they want, but they still won't be her.'

Unlike most of the population, Jennifer claims she hated the cut and even insisted on wearing a hat. More than anything, she hated the amount of attention it attracted. Flicking back through old photo albums, she cringes at pictures taken during the height of Rachel-mania. 'I don't like any photographs of myself. It's not me. It's definitely a different person,' she says studying press shots from the first series. 'Especially that Rachel shit. And with that old hairdo. I hate looking at those.' According to Jennifer, it was 'never a great haircut. It looked terrible on me... All I have to say about that is, "What the hell was I thinking?"'

An involuntary icon, Jennifer couldn't understand why people were so interested in her hair. She received hundreds of pictures from women sporting 'the Rachel' and while surfing online even discovered whole forums dedicated to achieving her look. 'This little girl online was like, "I just got my hair cut like Rachel's!"' Jennifer told her co-stars. The comment brought back memories of her own childhood. 'It's like when I got the Valerie Bertinelli cut, the coolest thing in the world. And I had all these burns on my forehead from my curling iron.'

But putting herself on a par with Valerie Bertinelli made Jennifer feel uncomfortable. 'It's very flattering to have people talk about your hair,' she confessed at the time. 'But I felt bad and wanted to say, "We all have different hair. Try something that suits your hair." Certainly, my hair wouldn't do in other styles. I wanted to tell them, "Even I have problem hair."' She didn't want to seem ungrateful, but if the truth be known Jennifer was desperately reaching for the scissors. 'I know everyone loves it. But I'm sick of it and I don't know what to do, chop it off or grow it long.' Such statements seemed like heresy, but true to her rebellious teenage years Jennifer went defiantly against the grain. 'It's just a fad; it will go away,' she shrugged.

But it didn't go away. The obsession ballooned to epic proportions and soon it became the dreaded topic of conversation in interviews. 'How do you feel about the hair?' mimicked Jennifer. 'What are you doing next with the hair?' Clenching her fists she winced, 'It feels nice, being reduced to a hairstyle!' Backtracking, she quickly corrected herself. 'Do I come across bitchy when I talk about it? I mean it's definitely flattering. It's also surreal.

It's like you start to become the haircut. Now I see all these negative things, like "Enough with her and her hair! I want her to just go away." I guess you can't let that stuff get you down or wonder why it's happening.'

Attempting to redress the imbalance, Jennifer went undercover online and posted a few comments of her own. 'I was saying things like, "I am so sick of hearing about Jennifer Aniston's haircut! Let's go back to what *Friends* is really about – the stories and the actors and not the haircut." It's just a fad. It'll go away. I do more on *Friends* than just flop in there with this bouncy little shag.'

Without doubt, this was one fashion trend Jennifer was fed up with following. But she couldn't really complain. The style eventually landed her a lucrative advertising deal with cosmetics company L'Oreal. Tossing her tousled mane in front of the camera, she whispered the famous catchphrase: 'because you're worth it'. Advertising executives obviously thought she was, as she was paid very well indeed.

Eventually, the studio relented and permitted Jennifer to ditch her famous mane. Relieved, she opted for a longer, sleeker, blonder look. Sometimes I lose perspective on how light I've actually gone,' she pondered. 'You go out in the sun and suddenly you're "summer blond". But it's fun to change. Michael Canale [in Beverly Hills] highlights my hair so well – he's got that touch, the natural touch. And, if I want to look funky, he won't do that. For a while I had dead, trashed burned hair – they ironed it so much for the show. I'm trying to let them go with my natural wave this season.' But with every small adjustment, Jennifer had to be prepared for a slaying in the tabloids. 'I'm always thinking, when I change it a little, am I ready for the beating I'll take in the press?' she sighed. 'You never get used to it. It always bruises your ego.'

Although Jennifer had always craved success, fame had never been a major ambition. A reluctant sex symbol, she tentatively posed for magazine shoots. A self-confessed ugly duckling at school, the idea she might one day be a pin-up was practically laughable. Proof of Jennifer's iconic status eventually arrived when *Rolling Stone* invited the actress to appear on the magazine front cover. Inside, a revealing photograph showed the actress lying down, with her naked bottom exposed. 'I was shocked,' she admitted. 'They promised there wouldn't be any rear end showing and then, oops – they went and cropped it wrong…'

The shots sparked ripples of excitement and disapproval from the public. 'I even had a woman stopping me in the street and saying, "Why did you have to do that?" Well, first of all, it's none of your business why I do something and for you to make a judgement on it is wrong. I get so livid about it; I'll sit there in the street and talk to a stranger about it for 45 minutes, just so there's one less person out there who thinks badly of me. But you know what? Fuck it and fuck 'em, I don't care. And, no, I'm not about to go and do *Playboy*. The centrefold is not going to happen. But I wanna hear the offers, so I can turn them down!'

Prior to *Friends*, Jennifer had been a relatively unknown actress able to go about her daily business without interruption. As *Friends* grew in popularity,

Jennifer noticed people would stop and stare at her in the street. Even the local shopkeepers, with whom she had casually passed the time of day, started to behave differently. At first, she dismissed the uncomfortable sensation as paranoia. But it soon became obvious this was more than just a figment of her imagination. People were starting to treat her differently. Slowly, it dawned on Jennifer: she was famous. All the daily chores she had previously taken for granted were proving increasingly difficult to complete. A trip to the local chemist, soon after *Friends* had aired, gave her a taster of what life would be like for the next ten years and beyond.

During a trip to San Francisco, Jennifer popped into a drugstore to stock up on toilet paper and a few beauty products. As she made her way to the checkout, she noticed a couple hovering nervously behind a rack of shampoo bottles. As Jennifer turned around, they apprehensively moved towards her. 'We weren't sure it was you,' exclaimed the woman. 'Would it be possible to have your autograph?'

Jennifer was stunned. 'I was standing there with my toilet paper under one arm and tampons under the other.'

While waiting for a response, the couple continued, 'We waited for you. We followed you.'

Apparently, the couple had been following her for several blocks, debating whether Rachel Green really was taking a stroll through their neighbourhood. Realising their request was pretty harmless, Jennifer happily obliged. But that moment was a definite turning point. 'When someone follows you 20 blocks to the pharmacy where they watch you buy toilet paper, you know life has changed.'

There were more weird encounters to come. On another occasion, a couple of star-struck fans approached Jennifer in a sauna! 'I was butt-naked!' she exclaims. 'This woman came up to me and asked, "Are you Jennifer?" I was like, "Yep, All of me. Every bit." It was such an odd place to meet someone.'

For the most part, Jennifer didn't mind dishing out autographs. As long as people were polite and didn't invade her personal space, she was more than happy to oblige. 'It's all part of it,' she reasoned. 'They don't know who you are at all. They know an image of you. You know you and you know your crappy side and good side and you know all that wraps up and makes you *you*.'

On the flipside, however, Jennifer could empathise with her fans. After all, she'd been there. Casting her mind back to the days when she camped outside record stores just to catch a glimpse of her favourite band Duran Duran, she had first-hand experience of teen obsession. Fame was something she would never take for granted. 'You know, it never really becomes normal to have people you don't know come up to you and profess their love for you and your work. It's amazing, really, when you think about it.' Given the option, however, Jennifer would have slammed on the brakes. Lacking confidence in her acting ability, she feared many of her accolades had been prematurely bestowed. 'Sometimes I feel like I still have so much further to go to be a better actor. You almost want to wait and save the fame until you're better at it.'

As the internet exploded as an information source, Jennifer found herself the focus of several websites. Curious as to what the public had to say about *Friends*, she logged on to several chat forums. 'It's always fun to see what everyone has to say. When I first started browsing, I became addicted! I would be on it until like 3am,' she confesses. 'I would surf the net and pretend to be someone else. I changed my name on an almost weekly basis. Sometimes I'd go into chat rooms and just see what people were saying about me. I walked in on plenty of conversations about myself. One person was saying, "I think I got rear-ended by Aniston."' Thankfully, Jennifer soon dropped the habit. 'These days I don't have the time to surf like I used to,' she smiles.

One of the strangest sites Jennifer stumbled upon was a religious cult based entirely around her person. The Holy Tabernacle of Aniston the Devine preached that 'God is a woman and her name is Jennifer Aniston' and that 'great hair is a spiritual gift'. Jennifer found the concept hilarious. 'I am not a god!' she laughed. 'But if I were,' she continued playfully, 'I'd be a nice god. Who'd want to be a punishing god? That'd be awful. I would love to sit down with all the people who are doing wrong in the world and go, "Hey. What's up with you? And what is your fucked-up problem? Go smell the roses, for crying out loud."'

Coming to terms with fame proved to be a struggle for every member of the *Friends* cast. Matt LeBlanc compared the phenomenon to 'hanging naked from a tree in the wind'. Jennifer had her own definition. 'My analogy is freefalling. It's like jumping out of an airplane, hoping your parachute is going to open. Doesn't everybody get a little neurotic?' Jennifer certainly felt the pressure of being thrust into the public eye. All of a sudden, people were rushing to note down her every word. A flippant remark could become a concrete newspaper headline within a matter of hours. 'It's a hard shift,' she said of her adaptation to life as a public figure. 'It's like learning to walk again. When you're a celebrity, all of a sudden your opinion matters. People want to know what your views are, so they better be damn good and make sense.'

Alongside greater expectations as a role model, one other major downside of fame was the inevitable tabloid interest that came with it. Photographers doggedly trailed cast members from dawn 'til dusk. 'People want to take a picture of you eating lunch,' complained Jennifer. 'What's the big deal there? There are people with fucking cameras at the bottom of the hill or when you walk out of a restaurant. Unbelievable.'

It seemed a telephoto lens lurked at every corner. 'It's strange with these videographers,' she shivered. 'They're like a silent eye, and it scares you. And I've seen footage of me that I was like "Where did they come up with that?"' Wary of prying eyes, Jennifer grew accustomed to watching her back. In restaurants, she would request the most secluded tables. During interviews, she would whisper cautiously. 'It's this whole loss of your anonymity,' she fumed. 'You never think about it until it happens, but it's a shock. Nothing you do is private.' Even worse, her love life took an unhappy dive. 'I'd try to go out on a date and there would be video cameras waiting. And, before I even knew if there would be a second date, I'd read that I was engaged to the guy. That guy wasn't calling back! Say goodbye to him!'

Desperate for a scoop, the tabloids linked Jennifer with numerous males. One of the more outrageous reports even linked Jennifer with a married wrestler called The Phantom. Even now, she finds the suggestion hilarious. 'I never met a wrestler in my entire life,' she exclaims.

While ludicrous newspaper stories still put a smile on Jennifer's face, invading her personal space was far less amusing. 'I was Christmas shopping, and at the end of a long hard day, I stopped at a coffee-bean place to get a frappe,' she recalls. After purchasing her drink, she returned to find her car surrounded by paparazzi. At the end of her tether, she reasoned a confrontation was in order. 'OK, look, just fucking talk to them,' she whispered under her breath. As she slowly edged her way around the car, the gaggle sheepishly retreated.

'What are you doing?' she asked.

'It's my job,' shrugged a shabby-looking guy. His nonchalance riled the already irritable actress.

'What do you mean it's your job?' she seethed. 'I understand it's your job, but you have no idea how invasive this is in my life. It actually makes me not want to do what I do. I mean, we go to work, we love what we do, and we do it for you, and we do it for people to enjoy. But if these are the repercussions – on my day off to see you with a camera in my face? I know it's your job, but you really need to think about how it's affecting people, 'cause it's just so disheartening.'

Jennifer was constantly frustrated by situations such as these. 'I've considered punching them out, they're awful people and I can certainly understand why Sean Penn would want to beat the shit out of them. They don't understand that they're ruining your life and they say that because you became famous you gave up your right to privacy. I did? Where was that written?'

Admittedly, outbursts of this kind were few and far between. At risk of being consumed by rage and paranoia, Jennifer had to keep her emotions in check. Impossible to leave, this was one inconvenience she'd just have to lump. 'It's hard,' she shrugged. 'There's a period when you just don't know what's going on. Suddenly, you have people camped outside your house and it's a little scary. Then you get angry and want your privacy. So you start to incorporate it into your thinking. You draw it into you if you're afraid of it, and you hide under the cap and the glasses. And then you just tune it out. I'm determined to live my life. I don't think about it much now. I'm a sloppy thing and go out not worrying how I look, but I'm not rude to people.' But very soon Jennifer was yearning to 'drive far away and find little antique stores and bed-and-breakfasts and go hiking... and just take some time out for meeting a man'.

In a very short space of time, Jennifer's lifestyle had changed dramatically. One of the biggest impacts was to her bank balance. Accustomed to thrifty living, she was stunned by the size of her pay cheques. Her salary rose from $75,000 an episode to $100,000 and eventually $125,000. 'That's not something I'll ever get used to!' she admitted. But she quickly made use of her newfound financial freedom. 'It didn't take that long, I'll tell ya!' she laughs. 'Ever since I was a little girl, I've wanted to spend money. Before my dad got the soap, we were broke. After that, there was all this financial shit with my parents and the divorce. So, once you get money, you're going to spend it. I was like, "I'm going to take my friends to dinner! Check's on me!"'

For the first time in years, Jennifer could splash out on lavish Christmas gifts for her family. She recalls giving her brother a Ford Bronco. 'He just cried. He was just like, "No way, no way, no way!" And he held me and wouldn't let go, and I felt his body trembling. For the first time, I saw this boy, this man, just lose it.'

Jennifer also treated herself to a few personal gifts – namely a 1970s Mercedes 280 SL. 'For an antique gorgeous car, it wasn't that expensive, although I'm not about to tell you how much!' she laughs. 'It's a tiny little thing. It's white and it's light and it's old and it kind of breaks down – it's a clunker, but it's really pretty... I still have a Land Rover too, but I mostly drive the Mercedes now – it's my new toy. It's been a fantasy car of mine for some time. I had the Land Rover before *Friends* even started, as I've always liked big trucks. Driving is such a pain in the ass that I like to feel bigger than everybody else.'

Responding to Matthew Perry's claims that she was a terrible driver, Jennifer scoffed, 'I'm an excellent driver, really. Although I'm sure that Matthew... would beg to differ – he said I was the worst driver in the history of drivers and that, if he knows I'm going somewhere in my car, he stays home. But he drives a black Porsche. It's tiny. Porches are a tiny little extension of a man's, erm, male self.'

As *Friends*-mania swept the world like wildfire, it seemed everyone wanted a piece of the show's six stars. One day, Jennifer was having her hair washed in the make-up room, when a producer's assistant mentioned that the Duchess of York was dying to meet the actress. 'Fergie?' she said, stunned. 'I like her!' Royalty and laymen alike, people couldn't get enough of the TV show. Those able to press the right buttons and pull the right strings even bagged themselves an on-screen visit to Central Perk. The likes of George Clooney, Richard Branson, Charlton Heston, Elle McPherson, Julia Roberts and even Fergie herself had cameo roles. A favourite with the viewing public, however, was a monkey called Marcel. The *Friends* cast didn't quite agree. Although cute in front of the cameras, behind the scenes he proved to be a menace. 'Well, I love the monkey...' says Jennifer, choosing her words carefully, 'when I watch him on TV. But, boy, that friggin' monkey could waste time on set. It could be cute, cute, cute then it would go into Outbreak mode, and we'd all be in trouble.'

One star who did make an impression on Jennifer was action hero Jean Claude Van Damme. 'No, he didn't make a pass,' she says, firmly setting the record straight. 'But he invited Courteney and I to his trailer to have dinner.' The girls graciously accepted his offer, but broke into fits of giggles at inopportune moments. They found his burly bodyguard particularly amusing. 'We were laughing so much afterwards. I mean, he was nice, but I can't figure him out. You just look at someone who's that huge a superstar and you wonder, Why does he have that guy with him all the time? Does he really have to have everything done for him? Does he do anything for himself? Does he do his own laundry? I'm fascinated by people like that. He didn't seem like a real person. I don't want to be quoted as saying anything bad about him but I think that European men like him have a weird way of thinking about women. I don't think he sees them as equal or people he can talk to. He thinks of them as playthings.'

Whether guest appearances boosted the show's ratings or simply the credibility of celebrities involved remained to be seen. Regardless, *Friends* had hit the jackpot. 'We were even number one in the summer re-runs,' recalls Jennifer. Cashing in on the brand, trivia books, calendars, mugs and all manner of memorabilia filled shop shelves. Jennifer was even amazed to find her face emblazoned on a packet of Russian-brand condoms. Wannabe comedians would recite the script verbatim and Jennifer's nonchalant catchphrase 'What-ever' would echo throughout school playgrounds and office blocks.

Audiences easily identified with the *Friends* characters, often imagining the actors must be exactly the same in real life. Ironically, this wasn't too far from the truth. 'I think that in my real life I sometimes think like a sitcom,' admitted Courteney Cox. 'My friends say that since I've been on *Friends* I've become funnier – I don't steal jokes from the show, but I get with the spirit of it.'

Matt LeBlanc agreed. 'We spend so much time building up the character during rehearsals that you get home and sometimes you haven't left the guy or girl behind. That's a little strange.'

Even Jennifer would confess that 'embarrassingly enough' on occasion she had reacted like Rachel in real life.

As the series progressed, the line between actor and character started to blur. 'Everything sort of morphs into one,' Jennifer explained. 'The friendships are very similar. The writers watch us and they get to know us and start to write in things that are similar to events that really took place. That happened with the poker-game scene because we were all obsessed with playing poker at the time. But there are lots of unreal things, too. David and I don't actually like each other at all! Seriously though, I remember the producers saying they never expected Joey to be so loving and warm. Matt just oozes those qualities and they've rubbed off. He's one of the sweetest people ever.'

In much the same way, Lisa Kudrow identified similarities between Matthew Perry and Chandler. 'They've taken a lot of Matthew and put it into Chandler – if any one of us is copied, it's Matthew most of all. He's got such an attractive style of humour that we all latched on to.'

But there was one actor whose on-screen alter ego happened to be a million miles from her own personality. 'Lisa is nothing like Phoebe!' stressed Courteney Cox. 'Lisa's really with it. She's so hot on doing impressions of people. Also she's a top university graduate. She's so smart unlike Phoebe.'

Each of the cast members had their own theories on why the show was such a success story. 'I think it represents, in this day and age, friends have become like a second family for many people,' suggested Lisa. 'People live more spread out from their families than ever before and their friends have come to replace them.'

David Schwimmer wholeheartedly agreed: 'Divorces are more common, more people go away to college or work abroad so families are split up. So you create another family out of a group of friends.'

But it was Matthew Perry who really hit the nail on the head. 'The good thing about friendships is you get to choose your friends, but you don't get to choose your family.'

Had Jennifer been given the option, however, she would have chosen to spend more time with her family. As work commitments grew, subsequently her free time evaporated. 'Unfortunately, I don't get to see my family and friends as much because I'm so busy,' she complained. 'That's a bad thing.' Jennifer had seen countless actors swept up by the Hollywood lifestyle and she was determined the same fate would not befall her. 'It's just a completely different world. People tend to assume you're different, so they behave differently. I feel frustrated a lot, not having the time to connect with people in my life who mean a lot to me. I just do the best I can. I'm fearful of becoming too wrapped up in myself and sort of unconscious, or not sensitive, of others,' she confessed.

Inevitably, during the first season of *Friends*, Jennifer saw very little of her old pals. 'For about a year and a half, she was so engulfed in this Beatles-like

A young Jennifer before she was catapulted into the world of the rich and famous.

Above: Jennifer with previous boyfriend Tate Donovan (*far left*), and the men closest to her; half-brother Johnny Melick (*left*) and father John Aniston (*right*).

Below left: Nancy Aniston, her estranged mother. Relations between mother and daughter remain tense after Nancy published her book *From Mother to Daughter to Friends* revealing intimate details of Jen's personal life.

Below right: Jennifer's godfather, Telly Savalas, was always a tower of support to his young godchild.

Above: Early in Jennifer's career she appeared in the TV adaptation of hit teen flick *Ferris Bueller,* playing the role of Ferris's little sister Jeanie. Pictured here with the cast (*clockwise*) Ami Dolenz, Charlie Schlatter and Brandon Douglas, 1990.

Below: Promotional shots taken from the television show *The Edge*, 1992.

Jennifer's big break came with the phenomenal hit series *Friends*.

Above left: With the gang *(left to right)* Matt Le Blanc, Courteney Cox, Jennifer Aniston, Matthew Perry, Lisa Kudrow and David Schwimmer.

Above right: The 'will they or won't they' storyline between Ross and Rachel kept the viewers hooked throughout the entire show right till the very last episode.

Below: A still taken from the show in the infamous coffee house, Central Perk.

The haircut that took an identity of its own. Initially known as the 'shag' and then the 'Rachel', Jennifer's wispy razor-cut hairstyle created a furore in hairdressers around the world.

"My Hair?
It's stronger.
It's thicker. It's new."

L'ORÉAL
ELVIVE
WITH CERAMIDE R

REVOLUTIONARY NEW SHAMPOO

Wash the **strength**
back into your hair.

Above: Jennifer's famous hair gained her a lucrative advertising deal with L'Oreal.
Below: The success of *Friends* ensured Jen made it onto the big screen. Here she stars in a supporting role in the movie *'Til There Was You.*

Above: In 1997 Jennifer landed her first leading role in the romantic comedy *Picture Perfect* starring opposite Kevin Bacon *(left)* and Jay Mohr *(right)*

Below left: Recognition for her acting talents on the big screen were to come from her next leading role in *The Object of My Affection*. The film received rave reviews and elevated her to the Hollywood elite.

Below right: With boyfriend Tate Donovan at the premier of *Picture Perfect* in 1997. After two years together, they decided to go their separate ways in April 1998.

When Jennifer met superstar Brad Pitt they became Hollywood's golden couple.

Above left: At the 51st Emmy Awards in 1999, clearly smitten with each other.

Above right: At the New York film Premier of Brad's film *Troy*, 2004.

Below: The marital house in Beverly Hills where their differing tastes were combined to make an eclectic and happy home.

phenomenon,' explains her Hill gang pal Kristin, who remained understanding throughout. 'Here she was in a show called *Friends* and we were her real ones. There was a period where we were hanging out, waiting for her to come out to the other side. And she did.'

However, not all of Jennifer's friends were quite so patient. Many were simply jealous of the star's success and looking for an excuse to put her down. But those who really cared lasted the distance and stuck by Jennifer all the way. Over time, Jennifer would successfully combine both her friendship groups. As luck would have it, there were already connections in place; Kristin already knew Matthew Perry and had directed a play starring Lisa Kudrow. Jennifer's high-school friend Andrea had also starred in a play with David Schwimmer. 'It just worked out!' says Jennifer with great relief.

Taking time out to spend with her friends, Jennifer organised a vacation to the ski resort of Aspen, Colorado. The 12-strong group of actors and writers holed up in a house on the edge of town. 'For years, we've been trying to get together, and the winter comes and goes, and we never do it,' Jennifer told pals. 'And this year, with *Friends* and everything, I was like, "You know what? I'm going to do this for us. Somebody's got to go ahead and make the plan." And that's what I did. And it's perfect. It's nice having the money to do it.'

Every day, the group would congregate at Bonnie's, a mid-mountain restaurant, before heading out for an afternoon on the slopes. At night, they would gather round an open fire and drink wine. 'I'm a cautious skier,'

Jennifer confesses. 'And then, when I feel good, I get a little crazy.... Very cautious to a point, and then I let it go – like dieting. If you're too strict with yourself, you sort of go off, go crazy, eat a pizza, whatever.'

In truth, the trip was as much a treat for Jennifer as it was for her friends. 'This is something she was dying to do,' revealed a close friend. 'I think she really needed a break; she worked so frickin' hard all year.'

Jennifer agreed her motivation had been partly self-interest. Caught up in a Hollywood whirlwind, she needed time to 'stop and ask myself, "What's up? What's real? What's going on?"'

Life in the limelight had many perks, but Jennifer was determined to remain grounded. Wary of falling under fame's fickle spell, she could distinguish illusion from reality. All of a sudden, sycophants would attend to her every need, but Jennifer could quickly weed out fair-weather friends. Rather than indulge herself in the attention, she preferred to stand back and appreciate fame at face value. 'It gives you a sense of power, but your life is always going to be your life,' she ponders. 'Sometimes it's hard, because it's easy to get swept up in the whirlwind. But it doesn't bring happiness; you know it's a game. A good game, but you learn lessons the hard way.'

One person who did keep Jennifer in constant check was her boyfriend Tate Donovan. A fellow actor, Tate was the star of American TV show *Partners* and the voice of Hercules in the Disney full-length animation. Years later, he would play Jimmy Cooper in the hit teen show *The O.C.* The couple met in a bar after being introduced by a mutual friend. Surprisingly, Tate had never seen *Friends* before but the pair instantly hit it off and arranged to meet up on a date. Jennifer remembers the occasion well. 'We went out for Japanese noodles and I don't even like noodles! There we were at a strip mall: I was all dressed up, he was casual. Tate had planned a low-key date to seem down to earth,' she laughs, before adding, 'But we had a great time!'

At heart, Jennifer described herself as an 'old-fashioned girl' who loved the whole tradition of courting. 'I have a problem with some of these Nineties men,' she would confess. 'I still believe in men courting women and I still believe in dates and I still believe in a man picking up a woman at her house and when you want to go steady you say, "Will you be my girlfriend?" I love that – I love tradition. I think it's quite romantic.'

Lost in conversation, the couple soon found common ground not only in their choice of profession but also past relationships. Tate's most famous ex was Sandra Bullock, while Jennifer had been on a string of dates with Counting Crows singer Adam Duritz. 'On our first date, all we did was talk about our relationships,' says Jennifer. 'We were like a mirror of each other. I was with somebody who was very closed down, and everything was always great, never a problem. If there was something wrong, he would never talk about it. I like to get rid of it. Why dwell on it, build up resentment?' Poor communication was one of Jennifer's biggest pet hates and the root cause of past break-ups. 'No communication is a bad thing that guys are guilty of. I hate men who are selfish with their feelings – men who can't talk about the way they feel.'

Jennifer found it therapeutic to discuss her past loves. 'I like to tell,' she says. 'You learned so much from those other people. It's half of who you are.' Learning from her mistakes, she had a clearer idea of the qualities she was seeking in a man. She described her ideal partner as 'a friend, someone who's equal, with whom you're comfortable... The ultimate is finding a place where you have no inhibitions, nothing to hide, where you can learn with one another.' Of course, there had been some unfortunate episodes in Jennifer's past but she preferred to learn from experience. 'Every man I've been with, I have to say, "Thank you for this lesson."' At the same time, she did not profess to be an expert on relationships. 'I am not a spokeswoman on relationships. I'm learning myself. Generally they've been great, but some suck.'

It was hard to believe, but Jennifer had experienced her fair share of dating disasters. The worst involved an incident in a Japanese massage parlour. 'This one guy was trying very hard,' she cringes, holding her head in shame. 'He took us to a Japanese massage parlour. We had a side-by-side massage with two Japanese women walking up and down our backs. I don't know why I ever got on the table. Maybe I was nervous. But it was disastrous. I never saw the guy again.'

Fortunately, Tate faired rather better and the couple clocked up a string of dates. 'He's the first man in my life to totally understand what I'm going through,' Jennifer swooned. 'After our first meeting, he called me as soon as I got home and we spoke for an hour and a half on the phone. I've never done that before.' But Jennifer was still reluctant to put any definition on their relationship. 'I don't know whether I'd call him a boyfriend,' she told pals in the early stages. 'Especially when it's so new and I'm so scared and sceptical and have been on this solo thing. Isn't that weird? I'm dating, and I like him very much. But when do I start to call him a boyfriend? Do you decide to go steady? You don't any more. Although Daniel, my old boyfriend, was funny. Three months into dating he said, "Will you be my girlfriend?" Got down on his knees.'

A serial monogamist, Jennifer had a history of long-term relationships. 'I've had serious boyfriends all my life,' she admits. At school, she was always popular with boys and never had trouble finding a partner. 'Guys liked to hang out with me,' she says. 'I thought because I had a quirky personality and was cute.' She started seeing her first proper boyfriend at the age of 14. 'We dated for a year and a half. Then, my high-school sweetheart lasted two years. After him, there were three years when I was alone. It wasn't until I moved to California that I had my first real mature relationship.'

The boyfriend in question was actor Daniel McDonald. Working mainly in TV, he appeared in several dramas and sitcoms. Most notably, he received a Tony nomination for his role in Broadway play *Steel Pier*. The couple split up just before Jennifer started working on *Friends*. Daniel moved to New York and his career took off. The couple remained friends and were always on hand to offer each other support. 'He's wonderful,' coos Jennifer. 'A dear friend.'

Even though Jennifer enjoyed relationships, she also valued her independence. During her single stints, she learned to enjoy her own space and company. 'I always found ways of entertaining myself. Men shouldn't be your whole life. That's what I took from my childhood – that I will never depend on a man as much as my mom depended on my father.'

Speaking about Tate, she said, 'I have a full life, he has a life of his own, and, if we can merge, terrific. But a relationship isn't going to make me survive. It's the cherry on top.'

A childhood spent in a broken home would have a massive impact on the way Jennifer chose to conduct herself in relationships. Nancy had several pearls of wisdom for her daughter. She advised Jennifer to 'be loved, happy, not to ever settle for something less than you deserve. Don't rely on men, but don't shun them, either. They're not your enemies.'

Jennifer explains, 'Of course, she was speaking from her own regrets about marriage. Discouraged and disappointed about the way her own worked out, but positive about it.'

A major strength of Tate and Jennifer's relationship was honesty and good communication. 'Neither one of us has ever explored that as far as we have now, and it's the key,' says Jennifer. 'That and respect.' Although her expectations were clearly defined, Jennifer was hardly a high-maintenance girlfriend. 'I'm not demanding at all!' she insists. The first time Tate brought her coffee in bed she almost wept. 'I couldn't believe it. I'd never had anyone do that for me before.'

There were more romantic gestures in store. When Valentine's Day came around, Tate took the opportunity to treat his new girlfriend to a special gift. 'I was shooting the show one night, and I came into my room during a scene and there was an Australian sheepdog puppy with a big red bow. My little Enzo. He's a good boy. He was a Valentine's gift from Tate.' To celebrate their first anniversary, the couple bought each other matching Irish Claddagh rings. During the summer break from *Friends*, Tate and Jennifer took off on a bike tour of Provence cycling 30–50 miles per day. 'It was great having a chance to clear the brain,' says Jennifer of the trip.

Further cementing the relationship, Tate even introduced Jennifer to his extended family. 'His parents are still together, he's one of six kids, and they were all really happy to see him,' she recalls. 'We sat around a big table in the house he grew up in. I envy that so much.' The visit certainly gave Jennifer a better understanding of Tate's past. 'I don't go for the big planned-out romantic gesture, but, when he showed me his old bedroom, it was pretty romantic.'

As Jennifer expected, the press latched on to her relationship with Tate scrabbling around for controversial stories. 'The money that people have made out of these tabloid papers and TV shows is unbelievable. It's the disgusting side of Hollywood. They're always making up fights between the *Friends* co-stars. There was one in *Star* magazine that said I was "The Queen of Mean". I was like "Whaat!?" Then they said I wouldn't let my boyfriend do an audition for a play because it would take away from "our time together". It was just awful. Another story said that I'd had a catfight with Sandra Bullock. [Allegedly the *Miss Congeniality* star trashed Jennifer's house, after discovering she and Tate were an item.] It was one big lie. I hadn't even met her, but I sent her flowers and a note saying: "I'm sorry." She sent me some flowers and, when we met at a wedding of one of Tate's friends, a couple of weeks later, we had a good laugh about it.'

Conducting a relationship in the public eye wasn't straightforward. Rather than allowing love to blossom naturally, impatient tabloids desperately tried to fast-forward the issue. 'It's a strange thing. All of a sudden on your second date, you're reading that you're engaged before you've even decided whether you want another date. It's a very weird thing, and that's why people cherish their privacy so much. Especially when they're starting a relationship. Because it's so hard to have a relationship, no matter what your career is. If you're in the public eye, that's a tough thing – especially when you don't know this person and you don't want to scare them away, because that can be very intimidating.'

Predictably, stories of phantom marriage proposals started to surface. 'That pissed me off!' fumed Jennifer. 'I only have to be seen in public with a guy and the engagement notices go in the papers.' Of course, marriage was something she'd consider, but in her own time. 'Marriage is wonderful. But I'm not desperate. I'm not itching for it. It's something that, hopefully, at one time in my life, I'll be able to do.' Children also figured on

Jennifer's future agenda. 'I've always said I'd like about three kids. I love everything about them. Their backs, necks, smell, all their fits. I want to be a young mom too. I'm not ready now, but in a couple of years...'

For the time being, however, they chose to live in separate residences in LA. Although Tate was eager to move forward with their relationship, Jennifer was more hesitant. 'We don't know, that's why I don't want to talk about it!' she told one reporter. 'But, when you're older and in relationships, everyone is a possible life partner. Your intention is not "Let's hang out for a couple of years and then break up."'

Although Tate and Jennifer had similar professions, both were able to draw a line between their professional and personal lives. While some men may have felt threatened by Jennifer's success, Tate was simply pleased for her. He even joked about their massive disparity of income. 'She's a lot wealthier than I am,' he scoffed. 'In fact, she's a lot wealthier than most people. You can actually be rich, and she'd still be wealthier.'

Mock rivalry aside, both parties were on hand to offer each other career support. 'There's no competition or jealousy,' enthused Jennifer. 'Tate understands what I'm going through. He's such a great actor. It's great to be so impressed with your partner.' Besides, Tate wasn't exactly living in his girlfriend's shadow. 'Tate hasn't stopped working since *Partners*. He's done two movies: *Murder at 1600* and this movie he just finished with Sam Shepard and Diane Keaton called *The Only Thrill*. And he's the voice of Hercules in the Disney movie. I just love that I'm dating a god.' On occasion, the couple would even run through lines together. 'I don't feel nervous in front of him at all!' insisted Jennifer.

At last, it looked as if Jennifer's life was really coming together. With a boyfriend to complement her successful career and healthy bank balance, the final piece of the jigsaw had been slotted into place. Reflecting on her current situation, Jennifer said, 'I never had an idea of what I wanted my life to be, like a picture I painted in my head. And your life doesn't stop happening to you. But, yeah, I'm the happiest right now.'

Chapter 7

Hollywood Calling?

While Jennifer had discovered many downsides to fame, there were also a number of benefits. Thanks to her higher profile, offers of work came streaming in. On the back of their small-screen success, casting agents were confident the *Friends* cast could become major movie stars. With the dreaded *Leprechaun* hanging around her neck like an albatross, Jennifer was desperate to wipe the slate clean and prove she could act. Incredibly, she still lacked faith in her abilities. 'I'm confident about some things, but I'm not confident about my work. I used to dread watching myself.'

Her high-school acting coach Anthony Abeson was far more confident. 'What you see on TV is only part of what Jennifer has to offer,' she says. 'She can go much deeper.'

Midway through the second series, Jennifer and her fellow cast members embarked on individual forays into the film industry. Although she would have preferred to secure roles on the merit of her acting talents alone, she had no qualms about exploiting available opportunities. 'What's good about being famous is being able to get a chance to do a project you love and think you're right for,' she reasoned. 'If I wasn't famous, I wouldn't have gotten the opportunity.'

Prior to working on any film roles, however, Jennifer undertook a couple of digital media projects. The first was a Windows 95 instructional guide with Matthew Perry and the second was a CD-ROM directed by Steven Spielberg and co-starring Quentin Tarantino, entitled *Steven Spielberg's Director's Chair*. While neither project was about to land Jennifer an Oscar, she relished the chance to hang out with some big industry names. 'It was unbelievable to talk with Steven and be able to discover what a wonderful, down-to-earth guy he is.' Admittedly, Jennifer was nervous the blockbuster director wouldn't live up to her expectations. 'I mean, you just never know. I'm sure we've all had our awful experiences of having idols and then you meet them, and say, "Oh my God, how could I have ever looked up to them?" And you wish you'd just kept them a figment of your imagination. And he was absolutely wonderful.' She was equally impressed with *Pulp Fiction* director Quentin Tarantino. 'I found it surprising that they could be so curious and interested in me. I almost felt embarrassed answering questions they asked. Steven Spielberg was fascinated by the whole television world.'

But it wouldn't be long before Jennifer could match her

expertise in the TV field with knowledge of the silver screen. Midway through filming the second series of *Friends* in 1996, she notched up her first credible film role with the Ed Burns independent *She's The One* (also starring Cameron Diaz). Jennifer played the part of Rene, married to a Wall Street whiz Micky (Mike McGlone) who refuses to sleep with her because he's having an affair with Heather (Cameron Diaz). He even compares the two women in terms of driving a '74 Buick against driving a brand-new Porsche. Casting Jennifer as a dowdy reject seemed improbable, but Ed Burns defended his decision on the grounds that using a glamorous and iconic actress to play Rene demonstrated just how spoiled and undiscriminating Micky had become.

Lacking confidence in herself, Jennifer felt apprehensive about taking on the role. 'I'm confident about some things, but I'm not confident about my work. I used to dread watching myself,' she admits. She was particularly conscious of the expectations imposed upon her. 'Because you're in the spotlight, there's so much pressure on you to see how you're going to do. Are you going to fail, or are you going to do good?' Even when Jennifer saw the final cuts for *She's The One*, she flinched with embarrassment. 'I was like, "I should not be on a screen that big. It doesn't work, it doesn't come across well." That was awful to see.'

Her director Ed Burns strongly disagreed. 'Everyone who's seen the film so far has been blown away by her performance. It's nothing like her character in *Friends*. The girl can act!'

More film roles followed, with supporting roles in *'Til*

There Was You with Jeanne Tripplehorn and *Dream For An Insomniac* with Ione Skye. But her first lead role came with *Picture Perfect*, a romantic comedy starring Kevin Bacon and Olympia Dukakis. Jennifer would play the part of Kate, a career-obsessed ad executive and reportedly managed to negotiate a $3 million fee. Her father John had recommended she read for the script, which was written by his friend and former *Days Of Our Lives* colleague Arleen Sorkin. 'When I got the script,' she says, 'I was still at that point where I was so overwhelmed by what has been going on in my life. I felt like I was free-falling.'

Eventually, the movie was made on the strength of Jennifer's interest. It was an indicator of just how powerful a commodity the *Friends* star had become. Eternally modest, Jennifer still couldn't believe her luck.

'When I told Jennifer that Kevin Bacon had signed on, she went, "I can't act with Kevin Bacon! I love Kevin Bacon!"' says the director Glenn Gordon Caron (responsible for cult 80s hit *Moonlighting*). 'She was so humble, so adorable.'

On her decision to accept the role, she says, 'There's that idea that you're supposed to strike while you're hot.'

According to the plot, Jennifer's character Kate is passed up for promotion because she doesn't conform to the 2.4 ideal of a stable married woman. Desperate to prove her company wrong, she invents a fictitious fiancé. She hires an actor called Nick and asks him to play along with the ruse. Initially, her plan is a success, although inevitably chaos ensues when Nick falls for Kate.

Jennifer easily identified with the film's themes, because

she remembered what it was like to be 'someone wanting to be different than who she was. Wanting to get out of a rut, and what do I have to do to make that happen?'

Her grasp of the script clearly impressed Caron, who commended the actress for both her comic timing and emotional sensibility. 'On some level, everything Jennifer does as an actor has to be with the business of being a human being,' he says. 'Jennifer exudes an extraordinary humanity, which you need to do this kind of comedy. No matter what kind of ridiculous or morally questionable things Kate does, you can always hear her heart beating.'

Jennifer described her character as 'a good girl who just went, "F*** it, I'm going to do something crazy." She takes some heavy chances and acts almost male as opposed to female in terms of doing something a little sly to get what she wants.'

Jennifer and Caron would spend hours discussing how Kate should be portrayed. Jennifer was keen the audience should relate to a woman misled by ruthless ambition. 'Kate made a big mistake but it wasn't her fault. She was thrown into this situation by chance... She could come across as mean and manipulative and a bitch and I didn't want that. I wanted people to have compassion and relate to her and get it. That's a hard thing to do, to ride that line.'

The script was never set in stone and Caron allowed Jennifer to make several amendments. One of her most memorable injections came in a scene where Kate walks into the bathroom, slams her handbag down in fury and shrieks, 'Shit, shit, shit, shit, shit, shit, shit, shit, shit, shit, shit.' Recalling the onscreen outburst, Jennifer laughs, 'Good line, huh? I came up with that one.' There were two shits in the script, but she improvised the rest. 'Nine of them were my shits,' she grins. 'I've made strides in my career.'

Before Jay Mohr was cast as Kate's love interest Nick, Jennifer had considered suggesting Tate audition. 'Tate would have been perfect for it!' she cooed. After some thought, however, Jennifer decided that acting alongside her real-life boyfriend could put unnecessary pressure on the relationship. 'When it's your first [starring] movie, there's an element of not wanting to have a relationship on-screen. That's where all the politics come into it. Eventually, we're going to do something together, because I'd love to work with him as an actor. But there's something about keeping your own identity and keeping your private stuff private. We understand that. No matter how perfect he is for that part – and he is – that's just not the way it should go.'

With many better additions to her CV, these days Jennifer prefers to gloss over *Picture Perfect*. At the time, however, she was proud of her accomplishment and quite rightly so. 'I'm happy with it. I'm not embarrassed,' she told journalists. 'I don't think it's a piece of shit, I don't think any actor should be faulted for taking a chance and trying something different.'

Caron recalls her initial reaction when the film was finished. 'The first time she saw the film, the 20th Century Fox logo came up, the drums and everything, and she said, "Oh, my God! This is a dream I've had all my life,"' he says fondly. After filming *Picture Perfect*, Caron was convinced Jennifer had all the makings of a Hollywood actress. 'Very few people can be funny and intelligent,' he pointed out. 'She's got the chops to be a wonderful dramatic actress. What makes her special isn't peculiar to youth. I could see her working into her sixties.' Commenting on her appeal, he added, 'If she didn't have the humour, she's so attractive, you'd be put off. But she's not the most beautiful girl in the world. She's, like, the second most beautiful girl. She's the one you'd go after once you realised you weren't going to get the most beautiful girl.'

Combining a movie career with a daytime job in TV was hard work. Juggling reshoots for *Picture Perfect* with her weekly *Friends* schedule, Jennifer found herself working from dusk to dawn. 'There was about a hundred things going on at once,' she frets. Comparing the two different fields, she says, 'They're so different. Working on a sitcom is, of course, the more familiar. The schedule is a lot easier, although the work isn't necessarily easier. But, like everything, if you do it enough, it becomes sort of second nature. Films are much more of a challenge. Besides the hours, your focus is much more intense. You're constantly tracking your character because you shoot out of sequence, as opposed to television, where you work from beginning to end.' Ultimately, however, Jennifer refused to choose between the two. 'I love them both.'

But the physical pressures of doing two jobs were often overwhelming. On several occasions, Jennifer almost reached breaking point. During these moments, she wished the world would stop for a day just to give her some breathing space. 'I just kind of went, "I can't do it.

I'm just a tiny little woman,"' she admits. Refusing to buckle, she picked herself up and soldiered on. 'I wanted my whole life to do this. And this is what it's about,' she reasons. 'I know there's lots of people who think, Oh, you shouldn't talk. You have a great life. You're making money and you're doing movies. And it's like, "Yeah. But you know what? I'm human, and shit happens."'

Aware of her shortcomings, Jennifer admitted that she'd bitten off more than she could chew. 'My eyes were a little bit bigger than my stomach,' she shrugs, considering the back-to-back volume of work she'd undertaken. 'You get an opportunity and you kinda want to strike while the iron's hot, and I said yes. Then I did another one right after that, and there was sort of a period where they were all happening at the same time. And I – I didn't pull a Mariah Carey or anything but, you know? I kinda exhausted myself. But, please – I'll sleep when I'm 80. It was so fun.'

Despite all of Jennifer's hard work, thus far reviews of her movies had been lukewarm. While critics never outright slated her efforts, the glowing reviews she hankered after were yet to materialise, although *Time* magazine did describe her performance in *Picture Perfect* as 'a nicely judged blend of intelligence and experience, briskness and softness'.

Still, she had been a lot more fortunate than most of her *Friends* cohorts. Only Courteney Cox had enjoyed any real success with the *Scream* horror movies, whereas the likes of David Schwimmer and Matt LeBlanc had made some ill-advised choices. Jennifer was extremely wary of making the same mistakes. 'You have to be very careful, because you want to make the right choice. You want to hang around for a while,' she says. Admittedly, Jennifer picked her career path carefully. But, when quizzed on the matter, she denied any forward planning. 'Someone is watching out for me, or something,' she says. 'I wish I could say that I had all these options mapped out and that I made these smart choices. But I was really just lucky.'

If Jennifer had been biding her time, her talents would finally be realised (and recognised) with her next full-length role in *The Object of My Affection*. Cast in yet another romantic comedy, Jennifer would play a woman who falls in love with a gay man. 'It's almost a true-to-life movie,' she enthused. 'I know women whom this has happened to – they know the guy is gay and yet they wish things could be different... What is also nice to see in this movie is a gay character represented as a human being. It's not a satire.' At risk of being typecast, Jennifer justified her decision to accept another romantic comedy, saying she was attracted to 'the characters and complexities of their relationships. In *The Object Of My Affection*, it's how they move through the conflict they're faced with at the end. It's a wonderful film, because it wasn't wrapped up in a perfect tiny bow. It was a gem, and it's hard to find those.'

At the start of the film, Jennifer's character Nina is dating Vince, a 'powerful, strong, ball-buster who doesn't demand much'. Then George (Paul Rudd) enters her life. 'He fulfils a whole new side of her that she didn't know a man could,' says Jennifer. 'I don't think she ever thought romantic love and friendship love could go together, and she gets thrown by that.' Jennifer easily engaged with the script and saw several similarities between herself and Nina. 'I guess I'm a bit of a control freak. I like order, but I don't think you can control when you fall in love.'

One of the most demanding aspects of the script was Nina's pregnancy. 'I really did feel pregnant!' she insists. 'The nine-month pad weighed like 13 pounds. So my lower back was definitely sore.... And it was a great excuse to eat M&Ms!' The experience also gave Jennifer some idea of what it might be like to have children. 'I'd like to be the perfect mom, but someone for whom it's OK to be flawed and make mistakes. We should allow for that and not shield a child too much. Let them know it's OK to run around naked and not be ashamed of anything, I definitely believe in allowing them to see the world as it is, but not exposing them to too much too early.'

Acting out a pregnancy proved a doddle but further challenges lay ahead – namely dancing. The film involved several complicated dance scenes and, although Jennifer could hold her own on a club dance floor she was certainly no professional. A choreographer was called on set to help out. 'I've got rhythm but when it comes to the steps I am just a white girl,' she shrugs. 'It's a tedious process. I wasn't great and I get frustrated so that makes it worse. You clown around and Paul's such a good dancer. It was impossible!'

But what Jennifer lacked in fancy footwork, she made up for in natural charisma. Co-star Paul Rudd found her near-royal status incredulous. 'People don't know her, but they do love her!' he exclaimed. 'People have the nerve to walk up and ask the most personal questions. The biggest testament to Jen is that she doesn't make them feel stupid for asking. She graciously responds.'

Perhaps the most bizarre display of public affection came from a girl who literally took the coat from her own back and offered it to Jennifer in the street. At the time, Jennifer was shopping with Courteney Cox on London's Oxford Street. 'It was so weird,' recalls Jennifer. 'I had admired her coat from afar and she asked me for an autograph. I casually complimented her on the great coat and she explained it was one of her own designs and insisted on giving it to me. She was literally taking off her coat in the cold and handing it over. I was mortified.' Although flattered, Jennifer felt uncomfortable accepting the coat and handed it straight back. Instead, she promised to visit the girl's fashion studio and buy one for herself. 'But she wouldn't hear of it!' says Jennifer. 'This went on for at least 20 minutes, by which time Courteney was like: "Hey, I'm not getting anything out of this deal! Can I have your blazer?"'

Ultimately, Jennifer's hard work paid off and *The Object of My Affection* received several rave reviews. From now on, critics would take the *Friends* star seriously as a Hollywood actress. She has very fond memories of the film. It's one of the few past performances she still looks back on with pride. 'I know what it's supposed to feel like,' she says, describing the experience. 'I don't think I did it before.' Previously cast on the back of her famous hairdo, at last Jennifer seemed to be wrestling free of the Rachel Green mould. Her confidence boosted, she was now ready to consider more challenging roles. 'On TV, you have an image and you don't want to limit yourself,' she told friends.

Along with acting plaudits, Jennifer took with her some extremely good memories from the film set. The crew enjoyed plenty of long-running jokes, the funniest of which involved Jennifer's obsession with farting. It all started when a make-up artist happened to play a tape of someone farting in the make-up trailer. 'It is sort of occasional,' she says, describing the sound 'and then it goes into like a symphony.'

Next up, Jennifer discovered 'fart in a can'. 'That pretty much took over the entire shoot,' says her co-star Paul Rudd. 'Everyone was obsessed. I don't care if you're a surgeon or a plumber – farts are funny, and they never get old.'

Even when Jennifer returned to her regular job on *Friends*, the fart jokes would continue. Her latest fascination was with a childish piece of putty, which Jennifer referred to as her 'fart sludge toy'. 'It's like this goo. You put your finger in it and it makes this noise … It's just the funniest thing in the world,' she joked. 'It was one of my greatest joys in life. I don't think I could have ever been happier.' Carrying the toy with her at all times, Jennifer loved to play pranks on unsuspecting victims.

'No one,' says Lisa Kudrow, 'does it as well as she can… It's a huge compliment. It's funny when she does it, because it doesn't seem very sophomoric – it seems very sophisticated. Because she's so subtle. It's fun to watch her go through her array of embarrassments.'

The gag continued for quite some time. Even Matthew Perry got in on the act with a remote-controlled fart toy. 'We were obsessed!' giggles Jennifer. 'You might not appreciate it, but it gets you every time.' Eventually, someone had to forcibly remove the piece of putty from Jennifer's possession. 'It was like, "Take it away, just get it out of her hands." Because I'd just do it and forget I was doing it in conversation,' she recalls.

It appeared Jennifer's career was going from strength to strength. With a reputable movie performance under her belt, a hit TV series to her name and work colleagues who practically constituted family, professional life couldn't be better. But, like any overnight success story, the *Friends* stars were about to experience a public backlash. The primary point of conflict involved money. *Friends* was ranked fourth overall in the US TV ratings and had become a UK hit on Channel 4. Naturally, the cast expected a reflection in their pay packets. Unfortunately, TV bosses weren't quite so forthcoming and the gang found themselves embroiled in several salary disputes.

Over the years, Jennifer's salary would rise from $22,500 to a breathtaking $1 million per episode. By 1996, when the sextet had three years of their original five-year contracts remaining, they were asking for $100,000 per episode. The NBC network were about to announce a $4 million syndication deal for the series contingent on the show running for five years. Aware the network couldn't clinch a deal without them, the cast first negotiated as a team and then individually. There were even rumours the cast might strike. Eventually, they agreed on $75,000 per show with incremental increases over the next few seasons.

Unfortunately, these uncomfortable financial wranglings were played out fully in the press, with cast members often branded as greedy and ungrateful. Journalists who had once supported the cast were now desperate to stick the knife in. Jennifer denied the sextet had ever threatened to strike and defended their actions saying, 'The six of us wanted to be paid the same amount because we all work the same amount as each other. The truth of the matter is that we all wanted it to work out the best way. And we knew that all of a sudden it became a media catastrophe. But you know what? This is how business works. Everybody negotiates. But someone ratted us out, and America got to see a whole aspect of our business that they didn't need to see. It sort of tainted our image... It was twisted into "Look at these brats demanding all this money."' After all, as Jennifer pointed out, the TV network would still make a financial killing from the show. 'They do get a bargain,' she argued. 'When you look back, *Friends* will, hopefully, be part of television history.'

But money wasn't the only problem. Alarm bells were also raised about the dramatic weight loss of the *Friends*' female leads. Both Courteney Cox and Jennifer Aniston appeared be shrinking at an alarming rate. Several journalists accused Jennifer of being anorexic and a bad role model for young girls. She found these comments extremely hurtful. 'I don't think I got thin. I think I got healthy,' she says, defending her early bouts of dieting.

'There was a point where I was sick a lot and my energy was low and I wasn't happy,' she admits. 'Then I started taking vitamins and exercising like a fiend, and maybe went too far on that, because you get in that Zone Diet thing and you get kind of addicted to that. But now I am kind of in a happy medium where I just do what I do. If I can work out, I do, but I don't go crazy. I'm just healthy.'

Resentment continued to grow. Tales of on-set arguments and oversized egos filled the papers. Magazines once instrumental to the *Friends* success story couldn't wait to break the TV idyll. 'Sometimes it seems that people can't wait to watch us fail,' Jennifer complained. 'It's strange, because you're doing the same thing on the second season of the show than you did on the first season – you're just trying to do the job… We looked at each other and said, "What did we do?" You take it very personally and then you learn fast that this is just the way it goes.'

A move into Hollywood only made the situation worse. Critics couldn't wait to ridicule cast members for their box-office flops, advising the ambitious troupe to stick with their day jobs. There was an element of truth to their cruel words. But it wasn't the amount of criticism that bothered Jennifer, 'it was more that people seemed happy about it… A lot of people are waiting to see if the Friends will fail,' she insisted. 'There's been talk about the other movies the Friends have done, and a lot of it seems to have a cruel angle to it. I don't understand why it's necessary.'

Egged on by the press, even the public started to turn against cast members. Fans who had once begged Jennifer for an autograph were now far happier hurling abuse. Whether on the street or in a restaurant, verbal attacks were becoming increasingly commonplace. For the most part, Jennifer refused to be baited by childish remarks. When pushed to the limit, however, she did lose her cool. One such incident occurred during a dinner date with a friend. Over the course of the evening, Jennifer became uncomfortably aware of a woman on the table opposite. 'She was eyeing me up,' insists Jennifer. 'I knew she was just waiting for the right moment to swoop in for the kill.' By now, Jennifer had learned to deal with over-familiar encounters with complete strangers. Having been beamed into people's living rooms once a week, arguably it came with the territory. 'People feel a certain level of comfort with you,' she reasons. 'They feel you're approachable. And the truth is I like to feel that way. When a kid comes up to you at a restaurant with a beautiful sketch he's just made of you and says he just wants you to have it, it's a real tearjerker. And I'm a leaker.' But this situation was different.

'I don't understand your life,' snarled the woman, a distinct smell of alcohol on her breath.

'Neither do I,' laughed Jennifer, somewhat taken aback.

'What's the big deal?' the woman continued, stumbling off balance.

'Beats me,' shrugged Jennifer.

'Look at you. You're normal. You're a bunch of nuthin', aren't you?'

By now, Jennifer was riled. This woman was both out of line and out of control. Edging forward in her chair, Jennifer snapped, 'What did you think? That I'm something? I never claimed to be something. I just do my job.'

For a moment, the woman looked puzzled. As if on cue, Jennifer's friend returned from the bathroom and moved the pest along. 'Well, I guess we'll go back to our nuthin' meal,' spat Jennifer sarcastically, proceeding to detail the incident to her pal. 'Tell me?' she asked, throwing her hands in the air. 'What was I supposed to say to her? "Sit down and I'll try to figure it out with you"?'

It was a difficult period for the stars. Abuse from the press became a daily burden that was impossible to ignore. Morale was low on set and tensions ran high. David Schwimmer summed up the general feeling: 'The experience with the media and the backlash we've felt has contributed to a loss of innocence,' he complained. 'I've gone through a loss of naivety that sometimes I wish I still had.' Equally, the impact was felt on screen. 'Ross has become less innocent too, and maybe that has something to do with me changing,' he continued.

Jennifer agreed. 'We're human beings and our feelings are hurt.'

Lisa Kudrow believed overexposure was to blame for the backlash. 'We weren't used to being actors who had choices,' she says defensively. 'We did a Diet Coke commercial, as a group, because the studio wanted us to do it, and Jennifer was the lone voice saying, "I don't think we should do that." She has good instincts, because after that there was nothing but negative press, pitting us against each other in terms of who was getting what movies and so on. We all got slammed, but we talk about everything, especially us girls, and we work through those things.'

For her part, Jennifer tried to rise above the accusations. 'We just keep going to work, doing our jobs. I go to work nine to five, come home, make dinner, order in, watch movies, read scripts, see my friends. It feels like I'm calm while that circus is happening outside.' She would spend hours analysing the situation, wondering how public opinion could switch so dramatically. 'We were just doing a job and loving it. It had great success, and we were thrilled. Then it got bigger and bigger, and then, out of nowhere, one day you're reading that people are really annoyed,' she shrugs. 'I guess a group of young actors getting a lot of money is going to piss some people off.'

Admittedly, the criticism knocked Jennifer's confidence. For a time, she became paranoid about her own forays into the film industry. Given the current climate, she feared any future endeavours wouldn't be given a fair trial. 'When it's time to step out and try something different, to challenge yourself, you can't help but feel this fear,' she complained to close friends. 'It's like you're not supposed to jeopardise your success by trying anything else. The compromise starts getting the best of you. Something that you loved from the time you were a kid starts to get lost.'

Jennifer continued along this path until her friend Steven Spielberg stepped in with some useful advice. 'This [backlash] happens to everybody,' he told her. 'Don't think you're so special.'

A survivor, Jennifer battled through. Sadly, the same

could not be said of all the *Friends* cast members. Reports were starting to circulate that Matthew Perry was suffering from exhaustion. His weight had dropped dramatically in recent months sparking numerous rumours of depression and drug addiction. After much speculation, it eventually transpired that Matthew was suffering from an addiction to alcohol and prescription painkillers.

Having known Matthew for years prior to filming *Friends*, Jennifer took the blow particularly hard. In truth, no one had seen it coming. 'It was so hard to be close to a friend and realise that he had been slowly killing himself,' Jennifer would tell chat-show host Oprah Winfrey. 'People would say, "Matthew looks really thin; what's going on with him?" We were with him every day, but we didn't get it.' In fact, it took almost a year for the cast to realise something was wrong. 'Matthew had always been the straight arrow,' she continued. 'He's not even a drinker! He's, like, a pure person. He made fun of anybody who got too drunk. He'd almost frown on you if you had one too many glasses of wine and were getting silly.' In the face of improbability, Jennifer had her own explanation for the breakdown. 'I'm sure it's a combination of a lot of things. Unfortunately, he's in the public eye, so his experimentation is out there, and I guess it went too far... It's a cliché. He was this beautiful, talented young man with everything ahead of him, and he still wasn't loving himself.'

Now willing to confront his problems, Matthew checked into rehab. Although well on the road to recovery, problems would resurface over the next few years. For the time being, Jennifer was simply relieved her friend was in safe hands. Defending his integrity, she played down sensational newspaper reports. 'I don't think of him as somebody who crashed and burned,' she said, when quizzed on the subject. 'I think he's sort of a victim of circumstances. He's doing unbelievably great and I love him all the more for what he's come out of.'

Could Jennifer ever find herself in a similar predicament? It was unlikely. 'We're different people,' she reasoned. 'Matthew is Matthew, and I am me. It's not my business to even talk about Matthew, but, speaking for myself, I know myself and I have an amazing support system, amazing friends around me.'

Fortunately, the public backlash didn't last forever. Rising above their critics, the sextet returned to the *Friends* set with new determination. Closer than ever, the cast formed a united front. 'Your life is suddenly under a microscope and it just takes some adjustment time,' said Jennifer, having emerged the other side. 'That's why the six of us on *Friends* are so close. We have each other to go to, to say, "Wow, are you OK?!" It happened really fast, and we try to make sure we're OK and to take care of each other.'

Putting the difficulties of the past year behind them, the gang were ready to move on. 'The show is still good. Everyone is so committed. We went through some troubles in the second year. Now we know we just have to stay true to our characters and the stories. For a while, we had a lot of celebrity guest stars, I don't think we needed to do that.'

HOLLYWOOD CALLING?

After a tumultuous few months, Jennifer's career appeared to be back on track. It was just as well. Over the next few months, her attentions would be diverted elsewhere. Little did she know it, but several major changes were about to take place in Jennifer Aniston's personal life.

Chapter 8

Love Heals

Ever since the show's inception, one of the biggest ratings winners for *Friends* was the Ross/Rachel storyline. Their on/off relationship kept viewers gripped every season. When the dream couple dramatically split, a public uproar ensued. 'It sort of ended because of emotional pride, not because they weren't right for each other,' said Jennifer, in explanation of the frustrating split.

The viewing nation was devastated – and they weren't alone. 'When we filmed our break-up scene last season, it was so devastating that it caught us both by surprise,' says David Schwimmer. 'I was actually embarrassed by how long it took me to recover from the first take. Jennifer made it so real.'

Jennifer agreed. 'That scene was so hard to film. David made me cry for real.'

Everyone desperately hoped the couple would get back

together. 'I hope they do,' sighed Jennifer. 'Only because I don't feel Ross and Rachel ended correctly. I think everybody knows that. It would be sad to see Ross and Rachel end because of some fleeting affair, because he was angry and she was angry. It was that love-hate-pride thing that separated them. As opposed to really knowing and making a conscious choice that they're just not right for each other. Which could happen too.'

Filming the break-up scene prepared Jennifer for some dramatic changes in her own personal life. After two years of trundling along casually, it appeared her relationship with Tate had run its natural course. After much speculation, the couple finally agreed to go their separate ways in April 1998. The specific reasons behind the split remained unclear. Some newspaper reports hinted that Tate was jealous of Jennifer's success, and sick of living in her shadow. Other reports suggested Jennifer was tired of waiting for Tate to pop the question. Jennifer vehemently denied there was any truth to the rumours. 'That wasn't actually why we broke up. But because we didn't give the press anything, they made it up. Tate's and my break-up had nothing to do with ego battles, wanting babies, not wanting marriage – all that stuff. None of it was accurate.' All she would say on the matter was, 'Everybody wants to be happy, but it's not the relationship's responsibility to make you so.'

Tate, however, pointed to irreconcilable differences in character. 'She likes top-notch hotels and luxury, and I like bed-and-breakfasts and riding my bike,' shrugged

Tate matter-of-factly. 'That's the most shallow version of it, but it's indicative of our personalities.'

There was never any animosity between the couple – over time, it simply became apparent that they were two very different people with conflicting outlooks and aspirations. 'I'm a New York City girl, and he's a suburban Jersey boy,' said Jennifer.

Although sad to lay the relationship to rest, Jennifer barely had time to wallow in self-pity. Little did she know that a new love interest was waiting in the wings, one who would change her life forever.

Jennifer and A-list movie star Brad Pitt had been introduced several months previously, but both had long-term partners at the time. The star of blockbusters such as *Se7en*, *Legends of the Fall* and *A River Runs Through It*, Brad had a string of high-profile romances to his name. Past girlfriends included Robin Givens and Juliette Lewis, while his current fiancée was fellow A-lister Gwyneth Paltrow. An international superstar, he was widely considered the sexiest man alive.

'Our managers wanted to set us up straight away,' says Jennifer. 'But it wasn't the right time. But the four of us would end up hanging out at a party here and there. I thought they were the loveliest people and he was the sweetest guy.'

As fate would have it, both couples went through break-ups at the same time. With both parties free and single, mutual friends decided it was time to make a move. Playing matchmaker, Brad's manager suggested the Hollywood hunk call up Jennifer and invite her out for a coffee. Jennifer was shocked to find the message in her mailbox. 'I was so nervous that I never called him back. The next day, I was leaving to film an episode of *Friends* in London, and he left a message saying, "Could I come up and help you pack and bring you some coffee?" I pretended I got the message too late. When I got back from England, we had a date.'

As it turned out, the date was a complete success. Conversation flowed freely and the pair found an instant attraction. Neither party could put their finger on it, but something magic was definitely happening. In the past, Jennifer had rubbished the idea of 'love at first sight' as romantic fantasy. Now she was happily proved wrong. 'I knew he was for me the minute I met him,' she grinned. 'He was just this sweet guy from Missouri, you know? A normal guy. I fell in love on our first date.' With retrospect, both Brad and Jennifer would agree that this was no ordinary date. 'We had a good idea. We had a good feeling, but you always have... you never know. But there was something, definitely something different.'

Although Jennifer had been in love before, the emotional avalanche still took her by surprise. 'Love looks differently,' she pondered. 'I think it has a different face each time.' Although she found it difficult to pinpoint exactly, Jennifer reckoned she'd been in love 'more than once' and 'less than five times'. Even though it appeared in many different guises, she could always identify love by its smell. 'The best smell in the world is that man that you love,' she swooned. 'It's like your dad. That smell of your dad.' Another of her father's traits she looked for in a man was his hands. 'My dad has these long, thick, beautiful hands!' She also loved the rough and rugged look, often championed by Brad. 'I used to love Nick Nolte and Jeff Bridges because of their rugged manliness,' she said. 'I love scruffy.'

Eager to develop their relationship, the couple quickly made arrangements for a second date. From that moment on, 'We were joined at the hip,' smiles Jennifer. In the early days of their relationship, the pair sought refuge in Jennifer's new house. Reached via a narrow winding road, the hilltop hideaway boasted fantastic views of LA, all the way down to the glimmering Pacific Ocean. The modest two-bedroom property decked out in antique furnishings lay secluded behind a giant metal gate and rustling orange and lemon trees. 'It was a little love nest. From the second date, we just huddled into this little house. We wound up sitting on the couch and ordering in, having steak and mashed potatoes. That's how it all began. It was one of those weird things where you just kind of know. You feel like you're hanging out with your buddy. There was something very familiar about it. This was just very much meant to be.'

Along with food, Jennifer and Brad also bonded over music. 'That's how we fell in love, really,' says Jennifer. 'All we did was sit at home and listen to music. We do have similar tastes – very eclectic in that we'll listen to pretty much anything. We also go through phases together. When we started dating, we were listening to a lot of Radiohead. They just sounded so good at that point in our relationship.'

For the time being, Brad and Jennifer were keen to keep their relationship under wraps. Both were uncomfortably aware of the pressures that accompanied a high-profile romance. 'You know, you want to live your life, and you want to have fun. You can't start something privately, you can't break up privately, you can't lose a parent privately – those are all the little thorns that come along with this beautiful rose. You kind of get a prick now and again.' Going on past experiences, Jennifer knew it was better to keep her mouth shut for the time being. 'Those are the things you kind of need to learn,' she said knowingly. 'Because when wonderful things are happening to your life, your instinct is to scream it to the world – whoever you are – that a wonderful thing in your life is happening. But there's definitely a price you pay for that. Because then, God forbid, that time comes around when you're no longer together.' In a worst-case scenario, media interference could even sound the death knell for a fledgling relationship. 'I remember, with Tate, they had us married before we'd even decided we wanted to go on another date!' In truth, Jennifer was under no obligation to share her private life with the world. 'My responsibility to the public is my work – not what goes on in my private life. To talk about a relationship trivialises something that's nobody's business. When it comes to privacy issues, it's a tough one, because I'm a talker.'

They went to incredible lengths to convince the media they barely knew each other. However, an incriminating photograph showing the couple nuzzling up to each other at a Tibetan Freedom Concert in Washington DC inevitably set tongues wagging. Jennifer refused to comment on the matter. 'Mm-hmmm. Yeah. They got a lot of legwork out of that one,' was all she would say.

Although representatives continued to deny any romantic tryst, the ever-prying tabloids were now on red alert, looking for any telltale signs that might reveal Brad and Jennifer were an item. The couple were spotted again at the wedding of Jennifer's close friend Kathy Najimy. Very quickly, the pressure became unbearable, but Jennifer reused to break her silence. 'It's something that I'm not even going to entertain or talk about,' she laughed, flicking her hair with feigned nonchalance. 'It's just one of those things that I just want to, as much as I can, not give it any weight, or give it anything, and that's hard to do. But I just don't want to talk about it. I can't talk about it. I'm sorry. I'm not withholding, just preserving something that's mine.'

The situation soon reached boiling point. Brad's new movie *Meet Joe Black* was due to premiere in New York. He and Jennifer had been holed up in the Four Seasons Hotel all day and were awaiting the arrival of their handlers. In light of recent newspaper reports, full security had been drafted in. Photographers had been offered six-figure sums to get a picture of the couple and would stop at nothing. Flustering agents and publicists mapped out the couple's moves with military precision. Brad would leave first in a limousine destined for the Ziegfeld Theatre. He would walk the red carpet alone and pose for the paparazzi. Any provocation from the press would be silenced with a dazzling smile. Jennifer, meanwhile, would enter the Ziegfeld Theatre via a back exit, accompanied by her agent Kevin Huvane. If the photographers did manage to nab any sly shots, at least she would be alone.

But the security forces couldn't work miracles. Despite Brad's attempts to keep paparazzi away from the movie after-party, several still managed to sneak in. When Jennifer arrived at the midtown Metropolitan Club, they were ready to pounce. They watched as she was ushered over to a corner table where Brad was waiting and received all the confirmation they needed when he greeted her with a long hug and a kiss.

Soon afterwards, Brad and Jennifer gave up trying to hide their romance. By now, it was a pointless exercise. The press had all the evidence they needed. In February Brad chose to openly host his girlfriend's 30th birthday party at trendy LA restaurant Barfly. Throwing caution to the wind, the pair even turned up together. Later that month, when Jennifer invited a journalist into her Hollywood Hills house, she didn't even bother to remove a picture of Brad from her coffee table. But she was still reluctant to openly discuss the relationship in public. 'I'll just tell you that this is the happiest time of my life,' she told reporters. 'That I'm happier than I've ever been. I'm not saying why, it's for a lot of reasons: work, love, family, just life – all of it.'

Jennifer needn't have worried. In this instance, there would be no unpleasant backlash. Although millions of women worldwide lamented the fact Brad was no longer a free agent, nobody could deny Jennifer her happiness.

Fans who had rooted for a Ross and Rachel success story now pinned their hopes on a real-life fairytale romance.

Fiercely protective of their pal, Jennifer's friends gave Brad the once-over. Fortunately, they fell in love with him instantly and gave the relationship their whole-hearted blessing.

'It's always been incredibly hard for us, always,' says Jennifer's close friend Kristin, 'because we've all been incredibly critical about men being worthy. All the men we dated had to go through an intense scrutiny process and I wouldn't have wanted to be any of them. They would walk into a room, it would all fall silent and you could just feel the stare.'

Jennifer recalls those suitability parades well. 'Oh my God, we were hard, very hard,' squeals Jennifer, 'and then, usually when there was a break-up, we'd get to unload. "I never liked him! Ever! I'm glad he's gone!"'

When she started dating Brad, Jennifer admits she was desperate for her friends' approval. Convinced he was definitely the 'one', she allowed their love to blossom in private before granting any formal introductions. 'It used to be, "I've met this new guy. Come and meet him and tell me what you think." Bad girl stuff,' says Kristin. 'But Jen kept this relationship very private, got very comfortable with it and made her own decisions about it.'

Eventually, Jennifer decided the moment was right to introduce Brad into her friendship circle. 'It was over dinner,' says Jennifer. 'We usually have a Sunday-night dinner. They all came over and they all met. It was a pretty instant love fest.'

Jennifer's friend Kathy Najimy sums up the group's response to Jennifer's new man. 'You go through a lot of different relationships with friends, but never was I absolutely positive like I was with Brad,' she says. 'I saw how much he loved her. I went home and I was weepy about it. She was 100 per cent herself with him, and that's all I really wish for my friends.'

Jennifer had known all along Brad would be a hit. 'My friends were all supportive – especially when they found out what a loving human being Brad is. At first they're like, "I hope he's not an asshole, some conceited fuck or whatever." But you get past that in five minutes, which is a real tribute to who he is. He just disarms you immediately. But, I mean, nobody went, "Dude. Brad Pitt!" and gave me a thumbs-up and a wink. They were just happy for me.'

Brad's friends were similarly approving of the couple. 'They just made each other really happy and it was completely obvious,' said close friend Catherine Keener.

Even Brad's ex-girlfriend Gwyneth Paltrow gave the relationship her blessing. Fortunately, Jennifer never felt intimidated with the past liaison. 'Gwyneth is a lovely person, but I didn't worry about their past relationship; it was never something that was an interference,' insisted Jennifer. 'Once this began, those previous relationships were done.'

On set, the *Friends* cast noticed a marked difference in Jennifer's behaviour. Love was obviously treating her well. 'Jennifer's a lot more peaceful now, like a woman who's in a good relationship,' said Lisa Kudrow. 'They [she and Brad] are both light-years ahead of themselves. You know how your grandparents have a certain perspective about life? They've got that now.'

It became blatantly obvious Brad and Jennifer were the ideal match. A mutual friend, director James Gray, was even amazed by their habit of finishing each other's sentences. The trio were having dinner together in a restaurant when Jennifer brought up the topic of Brad's smoking habit. 'Jennifer was telling him to wear his patch,' says James. 'She's trying to get him not to smoke, but she smokes.' He says, "Don't smoke either, honey!" and she says, "Well you quit first!" They're perfect together.'

In Brad, Jennifer found the emotional security she had always longed for. Although her parents' divorce was now a distant childhood memory, the implications would be felt throughout Jennifer's life. Brad was just the tonic she was seeking. He would supply Jennifer with a solid rock of support through some difficult times. Little did he know his services would be called upon sooner than he expected.

Relations between Jennifer and her mother Nancy had never been easy, but, as Jennifer's career exploded, they quickly took a turn for the worse. In February 1996, Nancy agreed to take part in a TV interview about Jennifer. She later argued producers had approached her to discuss the Waldorf education system, in which Jennifer had enrolled. For the most part, the interview went well. After a lengthy discussion of the school, the reporter moved on to a few questions about Jennifer's hair and her success on *Friends*. However, when the show eventually aired, the schooling system wasn't even mentioned. Instead, Jennifer's life story was the main focus.

Jennifer was mortified. She could barely believe her mother's audacity. Seething with rage she picked up the phone and demanded an explanation. Nancy claimed there had been a misunderstanding. Feeling betrayed, Jennifer swore never to forgive her mother.

Unfortunately, Nancy didn't learn her lesson. Two years later in 1998, she published a stomach-turning book, detailing Jennifer's childhood, her own difficult divorce and the breakdown in relations between mother and daughter. Entitled *From Mother and Daughter to Friends*, the book did little to reconcile Jennifer with her estranged mother. In fact, it only deepened the fissure in their relationship. Ironically, Jennifer had been on the brink of forgiving her mother for the disastrous TV interview. 'We got together once, and it went great,' insists Jennifer, before adding, 'except she neglected to tell me she was doing this book.'

Nancy claimed to have written the book in a last-ditch attempt to repair difficulties. Jennifer, however, interpreted it as a cheap shot at fame. It was bad enough having the paparazzi air her private life for public view – let alone her own mother! 'I don't think my mother understood how it would make me feel to have all that stuff broadcast,' shrugged Jennifer. 'But then, of course, when I told her, she still didn't get it... or she just didn't care how I felt.'

Try as she might, Jennifer's couldn't fathom her mother's motivations. Other than cause upset, what had she really hoped to achieve? Seeking explanation, Jennifer turned to her close-knit circle of friends. None of the gang had enjoyed easy childhoods. 'With each of us, well, especially me, Kristin and Andrea – our families are wonderful, but they definitely weren't easy,' sighed Jennifer. Sadly, these bonds only fuelled Nancy's resentment further. 'It was hard for them to understand these other people always being there – my mother especially,' Jennifer points out. 'I know she puts my life down a lot. She didn't understand how special and protective these people were. If only she knew, I think she would have felt less threatened and embraced them.'

After much soul searching and lengthy discussion, Jennifer reached the conclusion that she should cut all ties with her mother. It wasn't an easy decision to make. 'It's your family,' she said sadly. 'It's the hardest thing...' But, by dragging her daughter's private life into the public domain, Nancy left Jennifer with no other option. 'I'm a firm believer in keeping your dirty laundry to yourself.'

Her friends supported the decision. 'It's not like she woke up one morning and said, "I'm mad at my mom,"' says Kathy Najimy. 'She's really made such huge efforts to try to get it straight. But sometimes it's more productive to say, "Distance is going to heal this." That's where she is now.'

The whole episode left Jennifer deeply hurt. Every so often, she would break down in tears, wondering if she'd done the right thing. At these moments, Brad was on hand to offer reassurance. 'It's a tough one... I should have a shock thing around my neck like those dogs, when they start to bark,' she joked. 'When I start to cry, I just get electrocuted.'

Despite their difficult past, Jennifer and Nancy had been through a lot together. When John had walked out on the family, Nancy had single-handedly reared her daughter. 'The bummer is that we were so dirt poor when I was growing up, and now there's plenty of money, and I feel like we should be able to enjoy it together,' Jennifer sighed.

In recent years, Jennifer had been reconciled with her father, while her relationship with Nancy had slowly deteriorated. 'It's kind of ironic,' she said of the shifting balance in her parental relationships. 'My father and I are friends and my mother and I don't speak. I miss her. But I think this is a necessary break we have to take. Let it heal.' After her father being absent for most of her childhood, Jennifer now shared a closer relationship with him. 'My dad is just awesome, wonderful in every way.' After much discussion, Jennifer found herself able to forgive John for his parental inadequacies. 'He held himself accountable and said, "I apologise",' Jennifer explains. 'As an adult, how do you not forgive somebody who says he's sorry?' Now an adult herself, she could better sympathise with his predicament. 'He's a human being. We all make mistakes. As an adult, it's easier to see that than when you're an angry teenager going, "Why did you...?" Divorce, you know, is hard on any kid. So you kind of put everything out on the table, acknowledge it and be accountable, and move on.'

But some scars would never heal. When John made a flippant remark about not seeing enough of his successful daughter, Jennifer retaliated. 'Now, all of a sudden, you want to show up?' she fumed, partly in jest. 'This was your doing; you made your bed – you should lie in it.'

After her initial anger had subsided, Jennifer was left with a hollow feeling of loss. 'This is the last chunk of disease – dis-ease-in-my-life-my mom,' she told *Vanity Fair*. Later, she would vehemently deny any such statement. 'No, not at all. My mother and I are different people.' Thanks to her mother's foolish actions, Jennifer's life had been transformed into a real-life soap opera. 'Lord knows, I wish I had a different situation with my mom,' she wept. 'You know something, lots of daughters have difficult relationships with their mothers. Only when you're under a microscope, it gets played out in public like it's some kind of court trial.'

As the situation grew worse, Jennifer agreed to undergo therapy. But her visits offered little sanctuary from prying eyes. Even though her therapist worked from home in a quiet neighbourhood, the paparazzi still managed to track Jennifer down. 'You walk outside and there are four vans with lenses popping out!' she complained. 'They say you're an actor and it comes with the territory. But can somebody please tell me when I signed up for that? Whether you're a ditch digger or you're on a movie screen, shouldn't you have the right to sunbathe without worrying that some Peeping Tom is going to scale the wall to your backyard and take pictures of you? I'll gladly go by the rules if somebody would just tell me what they are!'

The more determined photographers even managed to track Jennifer's movements in her own home. Even an imposing iron security gate couldn't keep them away. 'I don't know how you can avoid those rascally paparazzi finding out where you are – camping out and doing that sort of pathetic existence that they do to fill those trash magazines,' she complained. Exasperated, she concluded, 'I, unfortunately, get a little too riled up by it. You're never going to win – so let it go and let it be.'

Thankfully, the actual therapy sessions proved to be much more successful. Jennifer dealt with unresolved problems dating back to her childhood. 'I'm still trying to understand those years of my life, and figure out what's real. As an adult, I can't blame my parents any more. At this point, we are accountable for our actions. We can change things.'

She surprised herself by the amount of sadness and ill feeling she managed to dredge up. 'You don't even realise it until you get a good therapist and figure all that stuff out!' she told friends.

Slowly, Jennifer tried to understand her mother's actions. Much of it undoubtedly stemmed from Nancy's own troubled childhood. 'I really do think my mother was trying to do the best she could,' she reasoned. 'Knowing the childhood she had, knowing the family she wanted to have – it just breaks my heart.' A victim of her own upbringing, Nancy was trapped in a vicious cycle she found impossible to break. 'We pass on diseases that we don't necessarily mean to... But my mother didn't know where she ended and I began. This separation needed to happen for both of us to find out.'

Even though she'd been through it a thousand times, the subject still brought tears to Jennifer's eyes. 'To feel that someone is so trying to live through me – it's a tough one.' But, although she could sympathise with her mother's situation, it was impossible to condone her behaviour. 'We all have our own struggles. Some lives are easier than others. It continues to be hard, but time will heal it. I know I love my mother, I will always love my mother, and we all make choices… That was a choice that she made.'

In the long term, Jennifer didn't rule out a reconciliation, but for the time being she refused to answer her mother's constant phone calls. The wound was still raw and wouldn't heal overnight. 'It's just a matter of time,' she sighed. 'I don't need an apology because I already know the truth, and if I approach her with an expectation of an apology it could just lead to disappointment. At some point I'll just have to let go and decide to forgive her, which I can't do yet.'

Unable to count on her mother, Jennifer learned to look elsewhere for unconditional love. By forming unbreakable bonds with her friends and work colleagues, she created her own surrogate family. With Brad's arrival on the scene, the final piece of the jigsaw slotted happily into place. Very soon, any sour childhood memories would pale into insignificance. Jennifer Aniston was about to embark on the most emotionally intense journey of her entire life.

Chapter 9

The Golden Couple

Having officially declared themselves to be an item, Brad and Jennifer appeared much more relaxed in public. However, both parties remained coy about the finer details of their relationship. Neither wanted to jeopardise their future together by encouraging potentially damaging rumours. But staying silent wasn't easy. 'When wonderful things are happening to you, your instinct is to shout it to the world,' admitted Jennifer.

At times, media interest was unbearable. For the tabloids, the relationship was a dream come true. Jennifer and Brad had repeatedly been named among America's 'most beautiful people' and the 'hottest Hollywood couple'. Reflecting on the public's obsession with Brad and Jen, long-term pal Kristin Hahn offered up an explanation. 'I think every celebrity is asked to be larger than life – beyond human,' she pondered. 'You have to be perfect in all sorts of ways. What we ask is mythic. We need people to admire and we don't have a king and queen; we have royal couples, and Brad and Jen are a royal couple. But they are very graceful about it.'

The world watched intently as Brad and Jennifer's love affair unfurled. Now everyone was rooting for a happy ending to the fairytale romance. A lavish celebrity wedding would be the ultimate icing on the cake. Rumours spread like wildfire. Where would they marry? What would Jennifer wear? Undisclosed sources claimed she would walk down the aisle in a Vera Wang gown, but wasn't about to rush into a spur-of-the-moment ceremony. As for a location, some suggested the slopes of Aspen while others pointed to the Chapel of The Quick I Dos in Vegas – in a scene reminiscent of Ross and Rachel's surprise on-screen wedding.

Jennifer's father John poured scorn on the rumours, complaining, 'I haven't received a wedding invitation!' But he gave the burgeoning relationship his blessing and didn't discount the possibility of a future union. 'Brad is a very nice young man, and whatever makes Jennifer happy makes me happy.' But, as any father would argue, no man would ever be good enough for his daughter. 'Of course not,' he smiled.

Jennifer's publicist Stephen Huvane responded to wedding reports with far greater ambiguity. 'One one-hundredth of a per cent of what's been written about Jennifer and Brad has been true,' he said, choosing his words carefully. Refusing to shed any further light on a future wedding date, he simply said, 'Assume they are a normal couple. Then apply logic to it.'

On 21 July 2000, the rumour mill went into overdrive when it was reported Brad and Jennifer would wed the following weekend. Brad's publicist Cindy Guagenti dismissed the reports, claiming the couple wouldn't be walking down the aisle 'in the near future'. Six days later, however, she went back on her word and revealed that Hollywood's favourite couple had set a date for 29 July.

To their credit, Brad and Jennifer had done a great job of keeping their wedding preparations secret. In fact, Brad had proposed five months earlier. 'That was so fun, just to have that be our own secret,' grinned Jennifer. But the couple had just three months to plan the ceremony. 'I knew it was comin', but I wasn't sure when,' said Jennifer. 'We kind of did it all in a three-month period. It just came to us one day that it was going to happen and we just jumped in and did it.'

Brad spent seven months designing her ring with jewellery designer Silvia Damiani, a diamond spiral that curled inward and continued outward – representing infinity. The Italian designer also supplied two white-gold wedding bands for the couple. Brad's was embedded with ten diamonds and featured the inscription 'Jen 2000', while Jennifer's featured 20 diamonds and the engraving 'Brad 2000'.

Jennifer would wear a dress by the Milan-based designer Lawrence Steele, dripping with tiny pearls. Her shoes were custom-made ivory suede high-heels by Manolo Blahnik. Her veil featured a crown interlaced with pearls and Swarovski crystals. To complete the outfit, she would carry a bouquet of Dutch roses. The bridesmaids,

Jennifer's friends Andrea Bendewald and Kristin Hahn, would wear pale-green slip-style dresses also designed by Steele. Brad, meanwhile, opted for a suit by Hedi Slimane, with his best man (and brother) Doug in Prada.

The couple would wed at sunset on a cliff-top in Malibu in a ceremony with an estimated price tag of $1 million. The couple rented the location, part of a five-acre compound, from producer Marcy Carsey (famous for *Roseanne* and *The Cosby Show*). There would be 200 guests (including high-profile stars such as Salma Hayek, Cameron Diaz, Edward Norton and, of course, the *Friends* cast), 50,000 flowers, four bands (including a Greek bouzouki band and French band The Gipsy Kings) and a 40-strong gospel choir. The ceremony would end with a $20,000 firework display over the Pacific.

Invitations to the event had been sent out weeks earlier, although the location had not been named. Guests were simply instructed to congregate at the Malibu High School, five miles from the wedding site. Minivan shuttles would transport them to the actual venue. One person conspicuously absent from the guest list was Jennifer's mother Nancy. She thought long and hard about inviting her mother to the wedding, but finally concluded it would be neither the time nor the place for a reconciliation. 'I can't believe I got married and my mother has never met this person I married,' she reflected after the event. 'I never would have believed it, when I was 17, if you had told me that would happen.'

But Jennifer was determined to remain upbeat. Nothing could ruin her big day. With the wedding fast approaching, she had enough to occupy her time. A team of workers were employed to prepare the space. Jennifer ensured everyone involved signed a confidentiality agreement, in a bid to keep details safe from the press. Anyone who leaked information would be liable for fines of up to $100, 000.

Tents and hanging lanterns were set up around the site. A canopied bridal walkway was also designed to keep the couple safe from prying eyes. La Premiere of Beverly Hills were entrusted with the flower arrangements. Roses, wisteria and tulips decorated the tables, while floating lotus flowers adorned a purpose-built fountain. Apparently, Brad had requested designers come up with a 'Zen garden look'. Jennifer's preference, meanwhile, had been for 'tons of candles'. Meeting her requirements, hundreds of brown sugar Thai candles were used to light the reception tent. In an attempt to keep the paparazzi away, part of California's Pacific Coast Highway was briefly closed down and the airspace directly above the property was declared an official no-fly zone.

As the day drew closer, Jennifer was overcome with nerves. Thankfully, those had receded by the morning of the wedding. 'I had those typical jitters the day before my wedding,' she admits. 'But the day of, I was just excited in a good way. The nice thing about weddings now is it's not just a chick thing. It's a team effort. The stereotype used to be men grumbling, like, "Why are you making me do this?"' In fact, Jennifer and Brad were both equally involved in the wedding arrangements. 'Brad and I were both so involved. It was a team effort and I loved it.'

The morning of the wedding, it wasn't only Jennifer who indulged in some last-minute pampering. Both she and Brad had matching highlights done at the Beverly Hills Canale Salon. Jennifer's hair was styled by Chris McMillan, responsible for the infamous Rachel cut. For her make-up, she asked *Friends* make-up artist Robin Siegel to do the honours.

On arrival, guests were served iced tea and punch and serenaded by a string quartet. The actual ceremony finally began at 6.30pm. Accompanied by her proud father John, Jennifer walked down the aisle to a six-piece band performing 'Love Is The Greatest Thing'. It was an extremely emotional experience and even Brad shed a tear. 'There's nothing more moving than seeing a man cry at his wedding,' cooed Jennifer.

Keen to personalise the ceremony, Brad and Jennifer had written their own wedding vows. Brad raised a laugh by promising to 'split the difference on the thermostat', with Jennifer promising in return that she would keep on making his 'favourite banana milkshake'. Later on, Jennifer missed her cue and turned to the congregation, joking that 'she'd never done this before!' In place of the traditional wedding march, a gospel choir played one of Brad and Jennifer's favourite Blur songs. She recounted the moment to *Rolling Stone* magazine, but preferred not to name the actual track. 'For our wedding march, we had this amazing full gospel choir play this song. Could you not say the song? It's such a private thing and so beautiful. I just want to keep it.'

To Brad and Jennifer's relief, the ceremony went

smoothly. 'All those horror stories you hear about weddings – the stress and the craziness – the whole thing was just free of that,' smiled Jennifer. 'I had heard of all the crazy things that happen to you when you plan a wedding; and, although we had some last-minute logistical things go awry, I've got to say that the whole experience was an absolute dream.' But she added, 'Of course, there were the normal freak-outs that you have before and after… You know, just the "Wow, we're doing this for the rest of our lives!" freak-outs.'

More than anything, Jennifer was glad to share the journey with her two closest friends Andrea and Kristin. 'It was an amazing rite of passage for us, with those two being my bridesmaids, my maids of honour,' she recalled afterwards. 'They are my girls and I just love them, and it was sort of profound and beautiful.' Not so long ago, Jennifer had played an instrumental role in Kristin's wedding. At the time, Kristin was seven months pregnant and incredibly hormonal. Had it not been for Jennifer, she would probably have turned up to the wedding in a tent! Thankfully, her friend was on hand to calm her down and offer good advice. She turned up with a beautiful wedding gown and four pairs of shoes. She even did Kristin's make-up. 'She took a good hour and a half, making killer Bloody Marys all the while,' says Kristin, forever indebted to her friend. 'In the end, Jen had five minutes to get ready, she didn't even care what she looked like. The music started and the only way for her and Andrea to get into the church was to come through the front and sneak past the altar.'

In the past 12 months, Jennifer's life had changed

dramatically. She never imagined that by the end of 2000 she would be a married woman. 'It's been a pretty fun year,' she smiled. 'Definitely deliriously fun'. She described her decision to marry Brad as the best decision she'd ever made. 'I love the feeling of being in love, the effect of having butterflies when you wake up in the morning. That is special.' And her worst? 'To carry on dating a boy called Robert when I was a teenager, instead of saying, "Sorry, this isn't working." It took maybe two months before I could pluck up the courage and that was two months wasted. You must say what's on your mind or you're not doing yourself justice.'

In this instance, Jennifer didn't waste any time. Having found her soul mate, she embraced married life wholeheartedly. Brad and Jen both had extremely fond memories of their wedding day. Alongside the traditional wedding photos, they had their own humorous shots. In one framed black and white photo, Jennifer is sitting on a counter in the bathroom. Only her legs (crossed and high-heeled) are visible in the foreground. Brad is in the background, sitting, fully dressed in a black suit and tie, on the loo. He's smoking a cigarette and drinking a beer. 'This is our Mrs Robinson photograph,' she told friends. 'It's a nice feeling to have somebody that you just like so much!

'I love the feeling of being in love,' she exclaimed. 'I don't know what it looks like, I just know how it makes me feel.' So how did married life differ to dating? 'Hmmm. It feels almost the same,' shrugged Jennifer. 'The most amazing thing is that now you have a partner in everything you do. It's a real gift when you find someone to share your life with... There's just some sort of deeper level of love and safety and commitment. It's wonderful. We keep saying to each other that it's like you get to play with your best friend for ever.' Jennifer would frequently cite friendship as the core of her relationship with Brad. 'You have to be friends first and foremost,' she insisted. 'That's the biggest thing. And that's what Brad and I are, and it's the best part of it.' Although Jennifer had enjoyed plenty of successful relationships in the past, nothing could compare to the magic she shared with Brad. 'This is the first time in my life I've been best friends with the person I'm with and that's a huge change... I mean, I've always been good friends, but there was always a part of me that never felt completely comfortable to go deep into that vulnerable part of myself. And that wasn't his fault, it was mine; I just wasn't ready. But in my relationship with Brad we've just been able to open that up for each other, organically.'

The way Jennifer described falling in love, it seemed like the most natural process in the world. 'It wasn't an effort, it was easy.' But it was far from plain sailing. Tracing back over their romance, there had been plenty of 'scary' and 'awkward' moments. 'Especially when you're in a relationship that's public and you're under a microscope!' exclaimed Jennifer. 'It's even more of a challenge just to remember that all of that is bullshit and we're doing what we're doing here and that's what's real.'

Coming from a broken home did little to dampen Jennifer's faith in marriage. 'I think marriage is a wonderful thing. I think if you're two independent people, financially and otherwise, and you want to celebrate your love, then you should do it.' Like every little girl, she had always dreamed of meeting her prince charming and marrying in a lavish ceremony. 'I have always been somebody that really wants to be married. And I don't know if that's just so I can do it differently than my parents did and prove marriage does work.'

As for the logistics of actual married life, she had few concrete preconceptions. After all, she had little experience to go on. 'I had no idea. I didn't grow up surrounded by any form of marriage... I never really had any dreams or expectations, so it has been far more than I expected and it has exceeded every expectation. It feels like everything that you felt, but more, and it's a commitment.' When choosing her future husband, Jennifer had just one goal in mind. 'I wanted it to be based in love, not money, not security. Just finding someone who was your best friend, who you could grow with and enjoy the passage of time – and that's what I found.'

By all accounts, Jennifer was a lucky woman. Journalists worldwide speculated on what it must be like to be married to the world's sexiest man. 'It's just funny to me. It drives him crazy, but I think it's funny. There's nothing wrong with that and they could be saying far worse things. It's all just silly fodder and you take it with a big grain of salt.'

But being Mrs Pitt did take some getting used to. The first opportunity to use her new name arose during a trip to the dentist. 'I was sitting in a dentist's office at seven in the morning,' she giggled. 'Brad took me to get my wisdom teeth pulled out. We were sitting in the waiting room and I'm scared to death and the woman opens the door and says, "Mrs Pitt" and we both went "Wow that's cool."'

Clearly, Jennifer was a changed person – and not just in name. Secure in her relationship with Brad, she seized the opportunity to look inside herself and exorcise the demons she'd been haunted by since childhood. Although cathartic, the process wasn't easy. 'This has been the hardest year of my life, as well as the best year of my life,' she told friends. 'The period after the wedding was extremely intense. This was the year I took the deepest look inward that I ever had and asked a lot of questions for the first time. There has been a real internal overhaul – about family, work, everything. Marriage brings up all the things I pushed to the back burner – the fears, the mistrust, the doubts, the insecurities.' Having tentatively picked at niggling problems in the past, now the floodgates were open. In the company of each other, there was no holding back. 'It's like opening Pandora's box. Every question comes out. It's like: "Here's the key, how about it?"'

When Brad and Jennifer exchanged wedding vows, they committed to each other for better or worse. Brad reassured Jennifer that he would stick by her no matter what. They were in this journey together. 'Brad and I said, "This is going to be a grand experiment – we expose ourselves completely. And that's what we did,' said Jennifer with pride. 'We said to each other: "We'll just do the best we can and be as kind as we can and as honest with each other as we can." That can be painful. But the only reason people should be together is to grow and to learn and to keep discovering and become better humans.'

Obviously, the experiment worked. Within five months of marriage, Jennifer claimed she and Brad 'knew each other better than either of us had ever been known before'. For the first time in years, Jennifer felt comfortable in her own skin. 'I'm just starting to feel I can stop apologising – to myself, to my family, to my friends, to the world – and live in my body and be OK with that.' Fed up with being a fixer, she could now lean on someone else. All her life, she had tried to make other people happy, to provide laughter in a household wrought with misery. Comedy had been her classic get-out card, but now she had a far more effective relief. For the first time, Jennifer no longer felt a pressure to be the 'good girl'.

Her weaknesses laid bare, Jennifer felt incredibly exposed and vulnerable. Brad did everything in his power to make her feel at ease. An emotional shock absorber, he removed the sting from every problem. 'It's been a real battle to get there,' admitted Jennifer. 'If I'm so concerned with eliminating shame and low self-esteem, there's also the thing about privacy: What do we have to hide? What do we have to be ashamed of? The bottom line is, I don't want to live that way. It takes too much energy. Who cares? There are certain things that are ours, and then there are certain things you feel – why not share? Getting married, taking that huge leap, asking yourself those questions beforehand... it was one of the most challenging periods. But, out of that, you're even more committed, more in love, more sure of your decision. It's a real trip, especially when you make the choice with your partner to live totally honestly together. That's the challenge.'

Together, Brad and Jennifer would share their most intimate secrets, fears and fantasies. 'True love brings up everything,' enthused Jennifer. 'You're allowing a mirror to be held up to you daily.' Through loving Brad, Jennifer was slowly learning to love herself. He could see past all her 'crap and dysfunction and insecurities and struggles. He kind of sees it through these beautiful rose-coloured glasses,' she smiled. 'I used to be concerned about what people thought – not wanting to disappoint my friends, my career folk. Brad taught me to love myself. I know it's said you should love yourself before you can be in a relationship, but, hell, I did it backward. I fell in love with myself as he fell in love with me.'

For the first time, she started to believe she really was a special person. 'If there's one thing I'm proud of, it's that I've finally gotten over not liking myself. It took me ten years to really notice, "Wow, you're not really nice to yourself, are you? You really don't like yourself very much." And then it took a long time to get to the point where I do like myself, but I actually do now. I'm a pretty happy person these days. I think too much, but, otherwise, I'm happy.'

Jennifer would forever be indebted to Brad for his kindness. 'He'll hate me for saying that, but, when you grow up in a family where people are not always very kind to each other, you realise how important that is.' But Brad gave Jennifer more than just love and affection. As a fellow actor, he also had a deep understanding of the industry and was able to offer his wife indispensable advice. In times of stress, he provided instant calm. On many occasions, Jennifer was able to return the favour. Thrust into the public eye, the couple learned to cope together. 'I think we learned it when we met. It's sort of trust in whatever the big picture is, and we'll remind each other. There are certain things that I'll get worked up about, whether it's being hounded constantly or whatever. I will let myself get too worked up over it sometimes, and will want to be the one who will change it. Yeah, like that's going to happen! Then he will ground me – we've got sort of a good balance!'

Since she could remember, Jennifer had always been driven by ambition. But now she realised there were plenty more important goals to be achieved in life. 'All of a sudden, your priorities shift a little,' she reflected. 'I've realised that I want to work to live, not live to work.' As much as Jennifer cherished her career, without Brad it would mean nothing. 'The ability to hold a job and do what I like to do is fantastic. But if the love wasn't there, if I didn't have this relationship... that would be a bummer.' In the fickle world of fame, Brad came to represent a pillar of stability. 'I know that we have something special, especially in all this chaos. In this nutty, brilliant, wonderful, hard business that we have, it's nice to have somebody who's anchored and knows you, really knows all of you.

'I'm proud of the fact that I've let go of the anxious attachment I once had for everything and everyone I cared about. Living is a daily process, and I've taken the pressure off myself. I used to say about my career, "This has to be the best. It has to be everything." I've lowered the bar so that my dreams are more attainable. I was having anxiety attacks, thinking, Who knows how long everything will last? *Friends* could be my last job.'

Even Jennifer's friends noticed a marked change in the actress. 'Success has changed her for the better,' said old friend Mandy Ingber, an actress and indoor cycling instructor. 'I think she has become more connected to her internal self. All the hype that's put out there has forced her to go inward, to look at herself and say, "What do I want?" Not just "What do all these other people think I am?" It always comes down to "Who am I – without this career, without this man." Once you get everything you've dreamed of having, you're once again left with yourself, and it's like an identity thing. Having what you want is almost as much of a question raiser as not getting what you want. Jennifer's journey is bigger than just being an actress.'

While Jennifer would happily declare her marriage to be a fairytale, she and Brad were prone to the occasional dust-up. Jennifer recalls their first fights. Frightened to let her guard down, she would flare up in retaliation. Looking back, she identifies it as a form of self-preservation. She was simply frightened of getting hurt. 'Marriage was hard. It rocked my world a bit,' she admitted. 'Every time I'd get deeper into intimacy, I'd realise that I'm in this for the long haul. I have to trust Brad enough to show me myself – my worst parts and my best. Right after we got married, there was a period when we fought, and I was like, "Oh no – what does this mean?" It just means you're fighting.'

A self-confessed conflict avoider, Jennifer was never one for shouting the house down. 'We have discussions,' she diplomatically explained. 'I am not a fan of fighting when it is screaming. I like accomplishing something.' Jennifer and Brad had their own method for resolving disagreements. 'I'm getting better at talking stuff out. I've gotten better over the past four years at doing that. We both said at the start, "Let's take everything we're afraid of and every problem and just face them head on." That means sitting down and saying, "That really bugs me" or "That really hurt me", and then you have some common ground and can discuss it. It's so much easier than to project it or to find something else to get upset about. You just go to the truthful place and it's not so scary. You just hand it over and if someone really loves you, they hear you. And then you talk it out and it's resolved. Done.' Besides, alongside loving, fighting was an equally integral part of married life. 'I don't trust a couple that says they don't fight,' she smiled knowingly.

Like anything worthwhile in life, a successful marriage required work. Neither Brad nor Jennifer was under the illusion that signing a wedding certificate guaranteed happiness. Both were embarking on a journey with a similar destination in mind. Jennifer explained it with the following analogy: 'This is an amazingly beautiful life but I look at life like rock climbing. You get through the first tier, rest a minute, look how far you've come – then you've another tier to climb.'

Chapter 10

Grand Designs

Compared to other couples, Brad and Jennifer argued very little. But one area of constant disagreement was interior design. Both parties had very strong and conflicting ideas on how their marital home should look. While Brad favoured modern aesthetics, Jennifer preferred the old-fashioned lived-in look.

Initially, the couple set up house in Jennifer's two-bedroom bungalow in the Hollywood Hills. Purchased eight years previously, Jennifer was extremely proud of the renovated Fifties-era home. She even kept 'before' and 'after' photos to proudly show guests. 'It's teeny, teeny, tiny. But it's my favourite place,' she smiled. The space was filled with family photographs and antique furnishings. 'I love antiques!' shrieked Jennifer. 'I love making something like an old tub into a flower holder.' Several of the furnishings had been fashioned from unusual objects: a glass-topped coffee table in the middle of the room was once a large gate door. It was hardly the home of a Hollywood millionaire. According to one visiting journalist, only a handful of designer sunglasses strewn across the table betrayed the owner's identity.

When heavy flooding buckled the hardwood floors, the couple and Jennifer's pet corgi-mix Norman were forced to up sticks and move to Brad's house half-an-hour's drive away. 'A pipe broke,' explained Jennifer. 'And we were trying to live on this rough terrain with all the floors ripped up. So we moved out here.' Brad had redesigned his house, a converted greenhouse, in rough-hewn stone, glass and wood. It boasted several high-tech fixtures, including stainless-steel toilets. From a distance, the place looked like an imposing post-modern sculpture. 'This is my husband's genius!' declared Jennifer. 'He doesn't have architectural training or anything, but this is his vision. He could go on and on and on. He keeps getting ideas so he changes something.' It was certainly impressive, but, if truth be known, Jennifer had never been a fan of the minimal look. 'It's hardly cosy!' she complained.

But, even by the time repairs on Jennifer's house were complete, the couple had decided it was time to sell up and move on. The flood had been a sign. 'This is only a two-bedroom house, and now we're spilling out of it. It's time to downscale and get the lives in one place,' said Jennifer. It was agreed Jennifer's house should go on the market, while Brad's place could be used as offices and an art studio. Jennifer had maintained a keen interest in painting and sculpting since her days at the Rudolf Steiner

School. Whenever her schedule allowed, she would retreat to the hills to pursue both pastimes. Brad meanwhile, would keep himself occupied with architectural pursuits. For her birthday, Brad presented Jennifer with guitar lessons and the couple were known to hold ad hoc musical jams with friends.

But finding a new property wasn't straightforward. 'We've been looking for a home, but we just can't find it,' Jennifer complained to friends. 'Do we buy land and build something or do we move into something right now?'

The couple spent three months searching for the perfect property. After much deliberation, they eventually settled on a six-bedroom mansion in Beverly Hills. According to newspaper reports, the renovated 1930s French Provincial-style property cost a whopping £13.5 million. Jennifer refuted such claims as preposterous. 'How expensive this mansion is? I'm not going to tell you how much it cost!' she told journalists.

Admittedly, Jennifer was sad to leave her old home behind. She had so many fond memories of the place. After all, it was within those four walls that she and Brad fell in love. She still referred to the place as her 'bungalow on top of the clouds. I'm having moving-on anxiety,' she shrugged. 'So many wonderful walks of life have come in and out... leaving it is going to tear my heart out.'

But with so much to plan with her new house, there was little time for sad reflection. At first, the couple had agreed to make a few alterations, but, determined to build their dream home, they soon decided to completely gut the place. 'At first we said, "We'll just redo the floor and the master bedroom." We ended up making the ceilings three feet higher, breaking down walls. It was symbolic of building our relationship,' said Jennifer.

It was a mammoth task, but neither was particularly fazed by the amount of work involved. 'Once we put the walls back together,' she said, 'I'm sure it will be a blast to decorate.' The actual renovations took longer than Jennifer had expected. 'Brad has such an incredible eye, and he gets in there and sort of says, "Well, how high can this ceiling go?" and "What's behind that wall?"' explained Jennifer.

'I love a construction site,' added Brad. 'I guess it's the possibility of what it could be... Playing within parameters leads to great discoveries – getting everything you want can actually hurt the project.' Further alluding to his passion for architecture, he went on to describe a building as 'a piece of art you get to walk through and experience. It drives me crazy.'

When it came to drawing up plans, Brad had some very strict directives. 'He definitely has strong opinions about aesthetics, and I admire that so much,' admitted Jennifer. But the pair did have different tastes and would often come to blows over the direction renovations should take. 'It's hard because the one thing I thought I could do well was put homes together, but it's something that really matters to him, so we've learned to make decisions that we both feel good about. And I actually think our marriage is even better now because we've been through this stuff. We've settled in; we've survived the whole house-construction aspect, and that's a big thing. It's not always easy. It takes work.'

Jennifer attempted to define their different tastes. 'He's more modern and streamlined about the future and I'm more Old World and classic. We kind of merged them together – a nice combo. He likes the structure and I like to fill it up. I do the inside and he does the outside.' Despite their disagreements, Jennifer was in awe of her husband. 'It's amazing to be with a man who actually loves that kind of thing. He has a talent for architecture and interiors that is mind-blowing. That's inspiring... he inspires me.' He even took her tastes and successfully melded them with his own. 'Brad has opened me up to a whole new world of auctions and antiques,' she said. 'I love deco, but I am eclectic. When I see a strictly modern home, I find it very cold and uninviting.' But Jennifer was grateful for his help. 'My sweet, dear husband, who has such patience with me, the idiot savant, is inherently brilliant with homes, structure. I had a hard time with it at first because I felt a little bit inferior, because, for me, it's not about the hippest thing, it's about what feels the best. It could be from a garage sale and, if it feels good, it will work.'

It was obvious Brad and Jennifer would never see eye to eye, but their ability to compromise was a credit to the strength of their relationship. 'The only time we've had disagreements is on design and house stuff... My home has always been my prized possession; it was always the thing that I did great... But that's all gotten so much better because we've realised we need to inch towards the centre to a common ground. And we have. We've been able to incorporate both of our tastes and make it a wonderful eclectic home. But there'll always be the moment of "No! That's far too cold. There's no warmth there". And he's saying, "Well, that's old and boring and that's been done." Then we'll fight it out and whoever doesn't have a bloody lip at the end... No, we're fine. It's all about compromise and I'm realising that's not giving up anything. There's a big thing about freedom and how no one's going to take that away. But compromising isn't giving up anything; it's actually about giving to someone. And I don't feel that's a loss of freedom any more.'

On another level, the process of building a house added a deeper level of intensity to their marriage. 'It was very symbolic for us. And we have a house that is truly a combination of both of us, and it's beautiful. At the end of it, it was the greatest thing we ever did,' said Jennifer, before pausing to correct herself, 'next to making a kid, and then the house will be the second-best thing we ever did.'

Ultimately, Brad and Jennifer were both happy with the end result. 'Our new house is great and I want to spend more time in it,' said Jennifer. 'We took some time moving in because we wanted it to be right. Brad even had the nursery painted green. It looks great!' If asked to choose, Jennifer struggled to single out her favourite room. 'I guess I spend quite a bit of time in our main bathroom. It is probably the most peaceful room.' The couple had chosen to forsake separate washrooms. 'We like sharing a bathroom. It's kind of where we talk.' But, whenever her female friends passed by, the group would always congregate in the kitchen. Whenever she and Brad walked through the building, they would always catch each other's eye and giggle. The project literally had been a labour of love.

In addition to the Beverly Hills house, the couple also purchased a sprawling oceanfront estate in Santa Barbara. Jennifer fondly referred to the property as 'Brad's Baby'. 'Brad's a land man,' she sighed, in mock exasperation. 'He wants land, land, land.'

For more than a year, Brad and Jennifer could talk about nothing but fabric samples and colour charts. But Brad insisted that would not always be the case. 'I don't think I'll do it forever,' he says. 'It's a younger man's game. I've got a few years left of a good run. And, truthfully, I'm interested in other things now. Like family.'

Once settled in their new home, Brad and Jennifer didn't want to leave. They would spend every spare minute at home, reading through scripts, watching movies or having friends over for dinner. The couple even enjoyed simply sitting at home and working in the same room together. 'We also play poker and look at design magazines. We're so boring.' Jennifer had never been a Hollywood socialite and after a long day's work she would rather hit the sofa than Tinseltown's hot spots. 'I just go home. I'll have a glass of wine, probably. Play with the dog,' she grinned. On several occasions, Jennifer declared her favourite night-time activity to be 'staying at home and watching sunsets, or kicking it after an evening with my husband – having a big bottle of water, reading a good book, and taking off my shoes'.

Although Jennifer insisted she was a dab hand in the

kitchen, often the couple would order food in from the delivery service 'Why Cook?'. When feeling particularly indulgent, they might order a Dominos Pizza, In-N-Out Burger or Taco Bell – Brad's favourites. 'We're order-in freaks... and creatures of habit,' grinned Jennifer. Often their only companion (aside from Norman, their dog) was the TV set. Surprisingly, Jennifer never grew sick of watching *Friends* re-runs. 'Oh yeah. It's actually hysterical. I love the show. I mean, that may sound really corny, but I do. We're flippin' through the dial and there's a re-run, and we laugh. It's fun.' Even before they met, Brad had been a big fan of the show. 'Brad's always been a big fan. He was slightly like a stalker!' Jennifer joked. 'He also loves *Will & Grace*. And he's addicted to *Survivor*.'

As for Jennifer, her preference lay with the classics. 'I love old movies,' she swooned. 'And I'll still watch classics like *Wuthering Heights* and get emotional every time, even though I have seen it so often. I like old TV shows too and Lucille Ball and Mary Tyler Moore are among my heroes. I think they are fantastic and stand the test of time. Their shows are still funny, mostly because they were so good at what they did.'

Happy in each other's company, the couple were self-confessed homebodies. 'I just potter round my house, turn on the computer and try to return e-mails,' confessed Jennifer.

In an interview with one British tabloid, Brad even defined the joys of marriage as 'being able to fart and eat ice cream in bed'.

'He told me he never said that!' squealed Jennifer. 'He

doesn't remember ever saying that. I was just like, "Why would you even tell people that?"' So, if flatulence and midnight feasts weren't the main perks of married life, what were? 'I would just say this amazing, overwhelming sense of calm and peace. It's like, OK, we've got that handled, we've got the love thing handled and now we can embark on life and the bigger issues in hand: how we can both better ourselves, better the world, spread love...'

Spending most of their spare time together, Brad and Jennifer developed an interest in each other's hobbies. Unfortunately, it was not always maintained! Jennifer had an unfortunate experience when she tried her hand at horseback riding. 'I made an absolute fool of myself and I will never get on a horse again. No, I will be getting on a horse again, but I won't be wearing flip-flops.' She recalls the incident. 'Brad, of course, can get on a horse and do everything. And I felt the need to show everybody when they asked me to come horseback riding – even though it had been 15, 20 years since I'd been on one. They gave me a horse whose leg had just healed after being broken. He had a very bad twitch when he came toward water. He would start to do a side step. It was insane. So we took this trail that had little dips and this creek and every time he saw the water, he would charge it, do a side step, charge into and Christ...!'

But horses weren't the only four-legged animal Jennifer seemed to have a problem with. 'Oh, there was a camel ride, too, but that was even more ridiculous. I end up being the comic relief, ultimately. There's nothing graceful about me and animals.'

Instead, Jennifer indulged herself in far more pleasurable pursuits. 'I love to take drives,' said Jennifer. 'I don't get to do it very often…. Or I get a massage and go to the hot springs… My self-help stuff is as simple as sitting and watching the sunset or taking a hike. Carving time out of my day to really do those things for myself and connect with nature. And reading. I'm always loving to read books on the self. I find it fascinating.'

Gradually over time, the couple learned to identify and understand each other's likes and dislikes. 'We're honest with each other and we do, I feel, bring out the best in one another. We're also not shy to say when we're not bringing out the best in each other. It's all very give-and-take in that way,' Jennifer proudly proclaimed. Brad came to love Jennifer even more for all her idiosyncrasies. It was hard to believe, but Jennifer did have her imperfections. 'I sleep walk,' she confessed to one magazine. 'I set our alarm off once, and I was outside. It was very weird. The alarm scared the shit out of me and I woke up, and I was out by the pool equipment in the back. I heard this yelling at me because Brad's terrified, he hears the alarm and I'm not there, and it's just awful.'

Although this was only Jennifer's second incidence of sleepwalking while living with Brad, apparently it was a habit she'd developed during childhood. 'There were a couple of times that my mom said that I would do that as a kid. I'd walk into the living room and she'd have conversations with me, and I would have no memory.' Thankfully, Brad supplied Jennifer with enough security to overcome her problem. 'It's so nice to be married to someone you like a lot. Brad is a nice man. He's considerate and good to people. I'm just so impressed with him.'

According to Jennifer's friends, one of her strongest attributes was an ability to appreciate the simple things in life. In spite of her success, she never once lost sight of reality. At heart, she and Brad were just a normal couple who were very much in love. 'She finds joy and beauty in small things,' said Kristin Hahn. 'She gets excited by a flower in her backyard. Most people let the gardener take care of that stuff. She is so grateful for what she's experiencing; that's why none of her friends resents her success. It's so easy to get lazy when you have everything at your fingertips, but I think that's why she and Brad hooked up. Each will make sure the other doesn't get lazy when it come to the important stuff that will matter when you're 80 and no one gives a crap. They challenge each other to have real intimacy, as opposed to getting away with what the world allows them to get away with.'

Jason Flemyng, Brad's co-star on *Snatch*, seconded this opinion. 'A lot of people who are that famous use it as a weapon to intimidate you, so you're never at ease. Brad and Jen know the effect they have and they negate it as quickly as they can. They couldn't be more generous; there's no status hierarchy at all. Lots of big American actors pretend to be nice, but at some point you're firmly reminded of who they are and you go, "Oh, fuck, here we go." With Jen, it's not like that. She's very proletarian.'

This much was true. Although Brad Pitt was an international icon, at home he was simply 'Jennifer's Brad'. It wasn't as if she woke up every morning in awe of the movie star lying next to her in bed, as other people might imagine. 'He can't get away with that shit at home. He's not Brad Pitt. He's Brad, pick up your stuff. He's Brad, shut the door. He's my Brad.' Brad, the sex symbol was 'everyone else's Brad... My Brad is lovely, sweet, good. He's doing what we're all doing: the best he can.'

Contrary to popular belief, Brad and Jennifer did not lead a glamorous lifestyle. 'We have a home base, and we've surrounded ourselves with friends. Our families, our poker games, our dinner parties – all of it keeps us grounded.' Unlike other celebrity couples, Brad and Jennifer did not live surrounded by opulence and grandeur. 'I don't mean it's not real, because it exists, and the industry exists,' reasoned Jennifer. 'But this idea that it's some glamorous, fantastic existence all the time – that's just not real. I mean, you go to work every day. It's like a nine-to-five job. You go get your coffee in the morning, you do your work and you come home. And then you gotta feed the dog, and you got your pool guy messing up something in the back. So there's all that stuff. I guess you could choose to go out, and partake and live in that scene. We just don't do that so much.'

Although they were never short of invites, the pair rarely attended glitzy celebrity events. 'It's so unbelievably unappealing to me, I can't tell you. I'm pretty boring in that way,' said Jennifer. 'We don't really go out. If a premiere comes up, we'll put on our fancy clothes and go, but those events are generally avoided at all costs.'

Rather than hang out with a bunch of famous acquaintances, Brad and Jennifer preferred to socialise with close friends and family. 'They both have a drive for success,' said pal Melissa Etheridge, 'but it never overshadows their drive for a healthy, happy life. They enjoy their careers, but if it was ever bad for them, they would so drop it.' Framed photos of loved ones filled the living room – 'me and my goofy husband skiing, my niece, my mother-in-law,' she said lovingly, lifting each picture up for examination. Guests would regularly drop by and evenings were frequently spent sharing laughter over games of charades, poker and even ping-pong! 'We don't take these games lightly. It gets pretty competitive!' insisted Jennifer.

Often friends would return the favour. During the summer, Brad and Jennifer would drive over to the Malibu house of Courteney Cox and her husband David Arquette. 'They just eat and talk and have glasses of wine and enjoy ourselves,' said Courteney. 'Once they spent the weekend. We pretended this was a hotel and kind of got away here.'

A couple of times a month, Jennifer would leave Brad at home and spend time with her female friends. She referred to the circle of friends as her 'source of sanity'. Usually the girls would meet up at a local Mexican restaurant for chips, salsa and a margarita. They would discuss anything from books, relationships and even Jennifer's latest tabloid headline. 'We sit around laughing at most of them!' said her friend Melissa.

Like any famous couple, Brad and Jennifer could never completely escape the paparazzi. It was partly the reason they often opted to stay in. When they did decide to leave the house, they simply took a deep breath and prepared for the photographers. 'And you may as well have on some make-up!' laughed Jennifer. Although when the couple purchased his-and-hers Range Rovers, Brad's was reportedly specially equipped with a rear-facing camera, linked to a database of paparazzi's number plates, to alert him whenever he was being followed. The fight against the paparazzi became a team effort. 'It can galvanise you,' said Brad, 'because you're in the fight together, and you get quite protective of each other.'

For the sake of her own sanity, Jennifer tried not to be riled by hounding fans and photographers. 'There is a part of me that understands the curiosity,' she shrugged. 'I mean, I was curious about famous people when I was growing up. I try to ignore the ridiculous tabloids that just make up a story a week, but it is irritating. You just have to try and keep your personal existence to yourself and your loved ones and protect your privacy as best you can.'

Jennifer appreciated the attention, but at times it did grate. She yearned for a vacation where she wasn't trailed my long-lens cameras. 'We have laws that are supposed to protect us from those things. It's unfortunate, and one of those icky parts of what we do. Growing up in New York and being mugged as many times as I have, I get scared when there's somebody following me and I don't know if they're going to be friendly or a psycho fan. You don't know. So that's the unfortunate thing, that I get just terrified.'

Her patience had snapped several years earlier in 1999

Making a conscious effort, Jennifer decided to choose movie roles that would challenge her acting abilities and showcase her versatility.

Above: With Jake Gyllenhaal in the low budget movie *The Good Girl*.

Below: A still capturing an intimate scene with Clive Owen in the thriller *Derailed*.

Doing what she does best. Starring in the hit comedy movie *Bruce Almighty* alongside Jim Carrey (*above*) and with Kevin Costner in *Rumour Has It* (*below*).

Above: With the *Friends* gang. Jennifer won an Emmy award for Outstanding Comedy Actress and *Friends* won an award for Outstanding Comedy Series, 2002.

Below left: Winning a Golden Globe for Best Actress in TV Series musical/comedy for *Friends*, 2003.

Below right: With Courteney Cox Arquette. Having met on the set of *Friends* they soon became best friends with Jen becoming godmother to Courteney's little girl.

Above: Filming the final episodes of *Friends*. It was a difficult time for all the cast members and an end of an era for Jen.

Below: Talking openly with Oprah on her show, 2005. Being a good friend of hers, Jen was able to talk candidly about her split with Brad and life after *Friends*.

Above: Jen bought this beachside bungalow in Malibu for some reflective time away from the public eye.

Despite the huge media interest in Brad and Angelina Jolie's (*below left*) relationship, Jennifer kept her dignity and poise. The devastating news that Brad was to become a father, shown here with Zahara and biological child Shiloh (*below right*), created an upsurge of support for Jen.

Above: A film still with Ben Stiller from *Along Came Polly*. Jen had to master the art of salsa dancing for the role.

While filming *The Break Up* Jen became close to her co-star Vince Vaughn (*below*). At the beginning the couple were very secretive about their relationship, even managing not to pose together whilst out in public. Here they are pictured with director Peyton Reed at a special screening of the film in Germany (*above right*).

On a day out, Jen is pictured with Vince at the French Open men's singles final, June 2006. After more than a year together, they decided to part ways in December 2006, but continue to be good friends.

Looking beautiful and glamorous, Jennifer wins the People's Choice Award for Favourite Female Movie Star in January 2007, a representation of her ever-increasing popularity.

when a crafty snapper took pictures of the actress sunbathing topless in the privacy of her own back garden. The pictures appeared in two magazines. After several heated discussions between lawyers, the lawsuit was settled amicably. 'You pick your battles,' she said at the time. 'I drew the line when someone crawled into my backyard and took a naked photo of me.'

Once the initial honeymoon period had subsided, Brad and Jennifer worked hard to keep the first rush of love alive. It wasn't easy. Comfort could so easily slip into complacency. 'You have to work at it because that honeymoon period is so intoxicating and so invigorating and, the truth is, that does go away,' Jennifer advised. 'But I really believe that there are so many other levels of intimacy that we have waiting ahead. But because rarely do we ever get to those stages, once the honeymoon period's over we just think, Oh that's over. That must mean it's gone. But it's always evolving and it's up to the individuals. And, if you really, really like each other as well as love each other, then it just comes.'

To his credit, Brad was never short of romantic gestures. 'He still helps me with my chair in restaurants and opens the car door for me and he brings me flowers and does all those fun things. He's a real gentleman, he's kind, he's generous, he's a goofball!' One Valentine's Day, Brad even had 1,500 red and pink roses delivered to Jennifer's dressing room. Jennifer was stunned to find every surface covered with flowers. There were even petals floating in the toilet. 'And on the mirror the petals spelled out: "I love my wife." That's pretty romantic, don't you think?'

Brad also showered his wife with gifts of jewellery; a diamond ring for her birthday and a necklace of three medallions. 'St Christopher for travel, because I am terrified of flying, one for success and marriage, and the third one is for fertility.' But Jennifer was anything but a high-maintenance woman. For her birthday, Brad took her bowling and then to dinner at a Mexican restaurant.

By the time their first wedding anniversary came around, Jennifer had forgotten she was ever single. 'It's just awesome. We don't feel like it ever was any other way. It's so true!' By the time of her second anniversary, Jennifer would declare that her marriage had exceeded all her expectations. She'd come this far, but Jennifer was loath to imagine her life ten years from now. 'I so don't think that way. I don't map out my life.'

It sounded sickly sweet, but Brad and Jennifer really were made for each other. An exception to the many fickle marriages in Hollywood, theirs was a love that seemed destined to last. Even Brad's unsightly beard passed the test of true love. 'You marry someone for better or worse,' she said, mock serious. 'I go through moments! I love it now because it's all soft and long and past the awful prickly phase. It's interesting. He's a chameleon and he can have so many different looks, and I just love him through and through, regardless of him looking like Kenny Rogers and a Unabomber!' Kissing was equally never a problem. 'I just love kissing him! He's the best kisser.' But, when the time came to finally shave it off, Jennifer was more than happy to lend assistance. 'I helped him shave it. We did all sorts of facial designs as it got less and less. There was the Amish look, the bounty-hunter thing, the French guy.'

They hoped and truly believed theirs was a love that would last forever. 'Once, when Brad and I were driving, we saw the sweetest thing: an elderly couple in a Toyota Corolla,' recalled Jennifer. 'They were both older than time, and I don't know how they were even driving. Her little hands were shaking on the steering wheel. Then he just reached over and touched her hand. It was a moment that seemed to say, "I've loved you for 70,000 years, and I still do." I hope that's Brad and me someday.'

Due to the nature of their work, Brad and Jennifer were inevitably forced to spend long periods apart. 'It can be frustrating dealing with schedules, but I have to say we've been really lucky,' said Jennifer. 'Brad's been working on this film in LA for the past year, so we've been together for the whole time and before we got married he never went away, except to do *Snatch* for a month in England. So we've really been lucky.' During that time, Jennifer visited Brad on set several times. She could barely understand the Irish accent he was forced to adopt for the film. 'I heard it the whole time he was shooting. He said, "Can you understand me?" I said, "No." And he said, "Good".'

Dealing with a long-distance relationship wasn't the only obstacle Jennifer faced. Her fear of flying also made it difficult to jump on a plane. But, when Brad was stationed in Malta to film the period epic *Troy* in 2003, she had little choice. He was away for six months, the longest they'd been apart since they met. 'Let me tell you something,' she said, shuddering at the memory of four separate plane journeys. 'That ain't no short trip.'

It was during one of Jennifer's visits that Brad experienced his worst injury while filming *Troy*. By now, the crew had moved to Mexico. While relaxing in their hotel, Brad and Jennifer were disturbed by paparazzi clambering across the rooftops. At the time, Jennifer was training on the treadmill. Brad reached over to peek to lift the blinds and accidentally caught his leg in the machine. 'We looked at the machine, and there was literally like an apple peel of skin with hairs on it,' he shuddered. 'It was gross, man. It's funny that my biggest scar on *Troy* was from my wife.'

When Brad was forced to travel for work, Jennifer would use the downtime to gather her thoughts. 'There's nothing like having some quiet time. But, I have to tell you, it's amazing to realise how much you love somebody when they're not there. Where are they?' Although she enjoyed the intermittent periods of reflection, she did feel lost without her partner. 'It is hard. It's a weird job that we do as actors, living like gypsies, and you need to have an immense amount of trust in each other. But you go and visit as much as you can on sets when the time's right and you know that you'll be back.'

Even when the couple were a million miles apart, they were never far from each other's thoughts. The director John Stockwell recalled how, on their way home from a Korn concert one night, Brad insisted on calling his wife at 3am. 'He wakes her up, but she's not mad, and he's just reporting in, not out of a sense of duty, but out of love,' said Stockwell. 'He's so in love with her, and I think he feels like he's truly hit the mother lode. In fact, I think Brad could never imagine cheating on Jennifer. I think he just felt like, there's no way – once you got her, you're not looking at anyone else... It is sweet. I mean, it will give you diabetes!'

George Clooney, Brad's co-star on *Ocean's Eleven*, equally upheld the relationship as a pillar of perfection. 'They're really fun,' he said of the couple. 'She'd come by the *Ocean's* set, and you look over and go, "Well, there's a homely couple."'

Brad and Jennifer eventually found an opportunity to work together when Brad gave a cameo performance on *Friends*. As a fan of the show, he had always been eager to put in an appearance. 'It had been on the cards for a long time as he got to know everyone through our relationship,' explained Jennifer. 'I have to say I thought the idea was really corny at first. Yuck! Pass the vomit bag! Then the girls on the show convinced me it was cool. And we all had fun.'

The executive-producer David Crane recalls the filming. 'It was terribly important to her that he have a good time and feel really good about doing it. It was really sweet to see just how much she was looking out for him.'

Although it was a fun experience, Brad and Jennifer both ruled out making a movie together in the near future. 'That's just asking for trouble!' said Jennifer. 'People wouldn't come to see the movie. It would be too much of a show in another way... It's hard when you think about how much of the microscope you'll be under. We couldn't just go out and do a movie, it has to be right and it has to be good. Maybe we'll wait 15 years, because right now there are so many silly little media circuses happening. Why add to them?' It would take a particularly strong project to pull them into the studio together. 'We don't want to put a big bull's-eye on ourselves.'

While Hollywood's hottest couple were reluctant to appear on screen together, behind the scenes they were more than happy to collaborate. Along with Brad Grey, they formed the production company Plan B. Together, they hoped to make a film about the life of Daniel Pearl, the *Wall Street Journal* reporter who was murdered in Pakistan. Initially, his wife Mariane had refused to sell the rights to her book *A Mighty Heart: The Brave Life and Death of My Husband Danny Pearl*, but changed her mind after meeting with the couple. 'She is one of the most inspiring and courageous women I've met in a long time,' praised Jennifer. 'And if the film is something that seems worthy of the story that she told, if it's done in the right way, then it will be made. That was sort of the deal that we all set with one another, as well as with her, because it's such delicate subject matter.' Jennifer was even considering the lead for herself. 'If it works,' she said, 'I would love to think that I could, but I reserve the right not to. We'll have to see when it happens. I'm just excited about nurturing it.'

Having set her own life on track, Jennifer eagerly turned her attentions to the world at large. In the past, she had made no secret of her desire to learn more about world politics. Subsequently, she and Brad became involved with One Voice, an organisation dedicated to bringing peace in the Middle East. But Jennifer was quick to distance herself from any overtly political action. She was simply interested in learning more about the world at large. 'We're not going to Israel. I'm hesitant about getting into a political discussion because I'm educating myself at the same time and it's so easy to take that and go, "Oh, they're going to Israel," and all of a sudden you're in the cross fire.'

In the space of a few years, Jennifer Aniston had become one of the most enviable women on the planet and it was easy to see why; she had the career, she had the house and, most importantly, she had the man. Now, only one thing was missing from her life – a baby.

Chapter 11

A Serious Star

While marriage had taken Jennifer somewhat by surprise, starting a family had been a lifelong ambition. Many of her close female friends had already given birth and Jennifer was starting to feel broody. She would often babysit her best friend Kristin's son, Boden. 'People always say, "Doesn't it make you want one?"' she said cradling the child during a magazine photoshoot. 'Well, you always do. You sort of know if you are a person who wants to be a mother. I always did.' That same afternoon, she burst into tears, simply contemplating the possibility of motherhood. 'I was just awed that this was Kristin's baby, holding him in my arms,' she explained. 'I just burst into tears. It was a heavy cry too; I wasn't quite sure what was happening. Very wild. Very wild.'

Jennifer was equally convinced Brad would make a great father. 'Oh, he'll be the best, a tremendous father.

He really will be because he's so kind and generous and warm, especially with children. I've never met someone who has such patience with children, like his nephews and nieces. With all of our friends' babies, he's just amazing, so I'm really looking forward to that so much.'

With a nursery already in place, the couple had grand designs on starting a big family. 'I love babies and I do hope to have a big family,' she admits. 'Most of our friends have kids and they seem to have a lot of fun. Of course, there is a lot of work and responsibility too but I still feel that babies are so magical that I want at least one of my own. Brad feels the same way.' Or, at least, that's what Jennifer thought. Brad famously told one magazine that he'd like seven children. 'Not unless he gets a mail-order bride,' was Jennifer's response. 'But I'll give him the rest.' Eventually, they came to a compromise. 'As we get older, we're downsizing a bit. As we're both getting up there, it's like, "You know what? Maybe three is good."' And, as Jennifer herself pointed out, she was 'born with the hips to make babies'.

With fans the world over eagerly anticipating a new addition to the Aniston-Pitt household, the pressure was on for Brad and Jennifer to conceive. 'There's no pressure from our families!' laughed Jennifer. 'I think they feel everyone else is doing it for them.'

Everyone had an opinion on the prospective birth – even George Clooney. 'It would be too much for Earth!' he smiled.

Every day a new story cropped up in the tabloids, suggesting Jennifer was pregnant. Did they want a boy or a girl? 'Either,' according to Jennifer. Had they decided on any names? 'Not yet. It's still early days.' And, above all, when was it due?

Although most media reports were in support of the couple, a handful of stories were both misinformed and hurtful. Jennifer was unfairly criticised for drinking and smoking after it was wrongly reported that she was pregnant. She later told the tabloids, 'We do want to have a baby. We will eventually quit smoking.' Most of the time, however, Jennifer was amused by the hysteria. 'I found the baby rumours hysterical,' said Jennifer in good humour. 'I didn't get mad. I got a lot of free desserts.'

So when would Hollywood's hottest couple become the industry's happiest family? While Brad was eager to get the ball rolling, Jennifer was more hesitant. Although convinced she could juggle motherhood with a movie career ('You can have a baby on one arm and a script in the other'), the ambitious actress preferred to wait for a suitable gap in her already heavy schedule. After all, there was no real hurry. 'Oh gosh. We have time, so much time,' she reasoned. 'Brad has said to me, "Listen, I'm ready now. But I'll wait. Two years." I'm like, "You're giving me a two-year window?"' In all seriousness, though, she didn't want to force the situation. 'If everything falls as it has done in the past, when the time's right, it will just present itself. We're not jumping in and trying to get any eggs fertilised as of yet.'

One such opportunity did present itself when Jennifer's *Friends* character Rachel fell pregnant in the show. 'We were like, "Well, jeez, we've got it written in here, it could come in nicely." But, you know, we'll see. All in good time.' But acting out the pregnancy had a profound impact on Jennifer and served as even greater confirmation that she was on course for motherhood. Tears streamed down her face as she cradled the newborn baby. The rest of the cast smiled tenderly, understanding how desperate Jennifer was to start her own family. As it turned out, she was crying for a very different reason! In a display of classic comic timing, she told reporters, 'Yes, I cried. But I was crying because they had smeared jelly on the baby's face to make him look like a newborn. That was what was truly disturbing to me. It had to be done, but the little angel was so good and quiet and didn't cry until cold jelly was smeared all over his face.' But she would later confess that the scene had moved her. 'The reality of the scene of Ross, Rachel and a baby – I just got sucked into it and it moved me. I am an emotional person anyway. My husband calls me a leaker.'

Eventually, Jennifer gave herself a deadline. Once *Friends* was finished, she would think about starting a family. 'I want to finish one chapter before starting another,' she declared. But already her priorities were shifting. 'You start to make choices. All of our friends have kids. Your priorities change, and it's about your home and enjoying the passage of time. Going to New York or Europe for five months isn't so appealing.' Brad and Jennifer had already discussed the changes to their lifestyle a child would necessitate. 'If it works out where we have kids, we'll sort of switch off. And the family will go wherever we need to go, which will be a nice luxury once *Friends* is done. But we haven't crossed that bridge yet.'

It wasn't just *Friends* that stood in the way of Jennifer having a child, there was also the question of her burgeoning film career. The offers were coming in thick and fast and, wanting to strike while the iron was hot, Jennifer didn't want to let any opportunities slip. 'At first, it was like, "A movie? Yeah! I'll do it."' she laughed at her own innocence. 'Before you even read a script! But you learn those lessons.' Her appearance in Mike Judge's underrated 1999 comedy *Office Space* was proof her skills of selection were 'getting better'.

Her next high-profile role was alongside Mark Wahlberg in *Rock Star*. In a bizarre twist of fate, Brad had originally been attached to the project (at the time it had a working title of *Metal God*). A year or so after his involvement fizzled out, the script resurfaced and the producers approached Jennifer about playing the love interest. They would write the part of Emily especially for her. Jennifer was extremely flattered and, on Brad's advice, decided to accept the role. 'I liked the story because it was about a fun period of the 80s. It's about this guy's rise to fame, what happens to him, how he adjusts to it, and how he handles it. I thought that was just kind of fun. It's all about fun, ultimately.'

Playing a support role also appealed to Jennifer. She wasn't yet ready to accept a lead. 'It's too much responsibility!' *Rock Star* also came along at a convenient time. 'It fitted into the time slot, and gave me free time at the end of the summer so I could breathe a little bit before going back to *Friends*. Which is always important to me.'

Creating a balance between her private and personal life was of increasing importance to Jennifer. 'How you choose to pass your time is very important to the quality of your life. Just this past season, I had just finished doing a film as I was wrapping up the last season of *Friends*. I was doing double duty, and it was so exhausting. I felt like something was going to suffer eventually. I'm not a workaholic. I admire people that can do so much work, like George Clooney. He was doing *E.R.* and *Batman*. I mean he was a superhero – I don't know how he did it. It's amazing to me.'

But there were other attractions to the project – Mark Wahlberg's involvement in particular. 'I love him, first of all. He's so talented, and he makes such an amazingly seamless transition from character to character. He's just good at what he does. Mark is that character. Like he put on those leather pants, and that was pretty much all he had to do. And there was no Marky Mark anywhere to be seen.'

Mark Wahlberg wasn't the only eye candy on offer. When producers told Jennifer her hero Steven Tyler might be making a cameo, she couldn't wait to sign on the dotted line. Aerosmith had always been one of her favourite rock bands. 'I don't know how old the man is, but he's phenomenal, that energy. He is the one person that Brad said I can have if the opportunity presents itself. He said, "You can have that one."' And who would Brad have in exchange? 'He's never said. It never comes up. Steven Tyler has just been our joke for a long time. I'm more verbal about it, I'm sure, than Brad is.'

Getting into character demanded a stretch of imagination from Jennifer. Unlike Emily, she had never pursued a rock 'n' roll lifestyle. 'I've seen a couple of shows in my life. But, no, I didn't do the rock scene very much. It kinda scares me, to tell you truthfully!' In fact, Jennifer claimed to be 'dull as they come'. Although that didn't necessarily mean she was boring. 'I mean, dull in the sense of the Hollywood scene. I'm not a dull person. You know what I mean. I've never gone down that wild, crazy road of sex, drugs and rock 'n' roll and partying and out all night.' But Jennifer was intrigued by life on the other side. 'I go out and play, but I'm talking about those people who are on the edge – and we've lost some of them.' Had Jennifer ever been to the edge? 'I've visited and maybe once stayed overnight.'

Jennifer scoffed at rumours she and Brad were closet potheads. 'That's a funny one!' commented Jennifer on the rumour. 'You read the headline, then you read the story and it says you smoke pot. It's not even cocaine or shooting heroin.' But Jennifer refused to confirm whether there was any truth to the story. 'I enjoy it once in a while,' she smiled. 'There's nothing wrong with that. Everything in moderation.'

Filming *Rock Star* gave Jennifer an opportunity to sample the dark underworld she'd missed out on as a teenager. 'If I felt I missed out on any of the wild times in my life, I feel like I've now had a taste of it,' she joked.

Brad gave her some great advice on getting into the role. 'Be Sting,' he told her. Jennifer explained, 'You know the way Sting's so sexy, so cool, and he's just there, he's just it, he doesn't have to try.'

For one scene, she was even required to kiss a woman during a dance sequence. Unnerved by the experience, she called on a shot of tequila for help. 'I'm so uncomfortable and out of my body doing something like that, so I had a bottle the size of an ordinary bottle of water!' At one point, the director Stephen Herek even pulled Jennifer aside and told her she had to relax. 'I was just having a hard time trying to get into the mindset of being affectionate, sexual, intimate, or whatever, with another person. So we finished that talk, he handed me that bottle and I was absolutely cured. One swig of tequila and I was raring to go.'

She loved transforming herself into a rock chick – it was a far cry from the good-girl roles she was usually presented with. 'It was a lot of fun. It wasn't the greatest decade in terms of fashion but it was sure fun. I kept a pair of leather pants and a pair of boots!' Fortunately, Jennifer escaped a dodgy 80s haircut. 'I think I made a point to say, "I'm not going to have bad hair, bad 80s hair." But it wasn't that great anyway. Emily still had the big bang.'

Despite all of Jennifer's efforts, *Rock Star* was critically panned and grossed only £10 million in America, against a production budget of £34 million. There was disappointment all round, but director Steven Herek was quick to commend Jennifer for her standalone acting ability. 'Jennifer is a very accomplished actress,' he told journalists. 'There are few people who possess her innate comic timing.'

Although *Rock Star* was a commercial failure, Jennifer was still pleased with her work. It was a step up from the run-of-the-mill movies she'd been saddled with in the past. A little wiser now, she was ready to switch up a gear and move on from the romantic comedies that had characterised the early part of her career. 'I'm tired of the cliché romantic-comedy formula,' she complained. 'But, if it's good writing and a story based in reality, I'll take a look. But if it's too much of a gimmick then I'm out. For instance, I'll get a script about a guy who pretends something in order to get a girl. Ugh… Things get thrown at you,' she reasons, '[but] there are only so many ways to tell a love story.'

More than anything, Jennifer desperately wanted to escape being typecast. Although she appreciated *Friends* had given her a springboard into Hollywood, she didn't want the character of Rachel Green to define her forever more. 'My fight has always been to get out of the Rachel shadow,' she sighed. 'Not to begrudge that because, God knows, it's been heaven… I have had this extraordinary opportunity to be on a show that allows me access to these films. Before *Friends*, it wouldn't have happened. I would barely have been able to get into a room to meet anybody… But, y'know, we're actors. *Friends* opened up a world of opportunities. So now it's "OK, what's next?" I'm excited to see if I can exercise different muscles. It's not that I don't enjoy romantic comedies. But give me a shot at something different.

'I'd love to do other kinds of films. A thriller or something. I love comedy but I want to evolve and challenge myself. It's easy to get stuck in what people are comfortable seeing you as. As you grow in the film world and become known, you want to mix it up a bit. It's hard

– you're under a microscope and, if you make a mistake, they go, "See, you didn't make it." But I'm an actor, I have to try something and, if it doesn't work, it's all right.'

Although she was now a bona fide A-list celebrity, Jennifer still lacked confidence in her abilities as a silver-screen actress. But she would never take anything for granted. 'I'm not sitting back saying, "I'm set for the rest of my life." They'll take it away as quickly as they give it to you in this business. There's going to be times, I'm sure, when I'll try something and it'll be awful and people will rip me apart, but I try not to listen so it doesn't intimidate me from taking the next leap.'

Jennifer made a conscious decision to be more adventurous in her choice of movie roles and to take educated risks. 'It's a very exciting time. It's been happening for the last two years – me saying, "I'm going to try this, regardless of what critics think." You can't help but feel bad when someone says, "Aw, she's nothing but a hairstyle." People say unbelievably mean things, but it can't distract me from what I want for my own self. And, if that means creeping along, not becoming big box office, like Julia Roberts, then that's OK.'

In no way did she expect movie offers to arrive on a silver plate. Although she was a massive TV star, she still had a lot to prove in Hollywood. 'I never have an ego about auditioning. I don't expect someone to think I can do something that they haven't seen me do yet. If I've never played the bad-girl part, I don't know if I can do it. I feel you either go in and audition and show them what you can do, or you get a job somewhere that can prove you are able to do it, so you have a piece to show a side of you that they have not seen before. You have to prove it to them.'

As far as Jennifer was concerned, she was far from being a movie star. 'That's someone successful in films, making millions.' But achieving that hallowed status wasn't an impossible goal. Deep down, Jennifer knew she had that unquantifiable appeal that differentiates stars from actors. 'I'd like to think I have that in me. I certainly have the desire. I don't want to be there because my press is more powerful than my work. I want to have a body of work where I feel proud to say, "Now I feel like I've earned this label of movie star." And, eventually, I will.'

Jennifer finally found her chance to shine when she appeared in the independent movie *The Good Girl*. Not only did Jennifer take a massive pay cut to appear in the low-budget movie, but she also ditched her glamorous image to play a depressed housewife. Fed up with her job in Retail Rodeo, a small-town Texan discount store, and irritated by her lazy pot-smoking husband, her character Justine embarks on a disastrous affair with a young troubled colleague, played by 21-year-old Jake Gyllenhaal.

Screenwriter Mike White came up with the idea of casting Jennifer in such an unusual role. 'I thought it would be fresh – who wouldn't want to see America's sweetheart get blackmailed for sex, try to institutionalise her boyfriend and cheat on her husband?'

The director Miguel Arteta followed up White's suggestion. 'Ten years ago, I got to meet my favourite director, Sam Fuller, for about two hours,' he recalled. 'He would come right up to my face with his cigar, and say, "Cast on hunch, kid! Cast your neighbour, cast the biggest movie star in the world. Just cast on hunch!" When Mike suggested Jennifer Aniston, I remembered Sam's face. Not only did it seem mischievous and fun, it gave a whole new look to the film.'

Others were less enthusiastic. 'I'd heard of her, obviously, and her haircut surrounded me for a couple of years when every girl had it,' said co-star Reilly. 'But I was like, "Jennifer Aniston? That girl on the TV show? Wait, explain that to me."' But, after working with Jennifer, he soon changed his tune. 'She's the real deal, just real ordinary. She put to rest whatever questions people had.'

When the script initially arrived in Jennifer's lap, she thought there must have been some sort of mistake. 'I read it in an hour. The writer, Mike White, has an ability to create characters that are so creepy and dysfunctional and human, with this duality that makes people feel empathy for them at the same time.' Jennifer recognised this as the opportunity she'd been waiting for. 'The story was something I wanted to be a part of telling, and the character was so multidimensional that it was impossible for me to say no. The budget isn't something that plays a large role in whether I do a film. The story, director and other actors are what I look for.' But she still found it hard to believe the producers would even consider her for the part. 'My first thought was: Was this sent to the right person? I called my agent. "Are they sure? Let's say yes before they realise they've sent it to the wrong person!"' Jennifer was instantly cast without audition.

Jennifer enjoyed the challenge of taking on a role so far removed from her usual repertoire. 'I've always been on the comedic side because it was a safe haven and it made me feel good, so it was a challenge to explore a different side of myself – a side that is sometimes sad, dark and depressed.' Jennifer filmed *Friends* and *The Good Girl* concurrently and enjoyed the massive disparity between roles. 'It was exciting to not wear all the pounds of make-up, blow dry your hair and all that stuff. I felt like I've been waiting for this all my life.'

But Jennifer was under no illusions. Given her background, she would have to work twice as hard to prove herself. She could already sense the critics were sharpening their swords and preparing to attack. 'You can't blame people for not trusting me to be able to do something,' she acknowledged. 'Just because you can do one thing really well doesn't mean you can score at everything else. So it's up to me to kind of prove myself, and I don't mind that.' Of course, there was a risk Jennifer might not be ready to make the transition to serious cinema, but she couldn't pass up the opportunity. 'I kind of felt like, if I'm going to sink or sail, I better try it now. What the hell. I've got nothing to lose. It can't be worse than *Leprechaun*.'

Her agent Kevin Huvane agreed the film was a good move. 'People who do comedy are always underrated because they make it look so easy, so it was exciting to see Jen challenge herself with a film like *The Good Girl* – which is pretty much the antithesis of *Friends* – and get the sort of recognition she deserves. I don't think there's any limit to what she can do.'

From the minute Jennifer stepped on set, Arteta was impressed with her portrayal. Without a shadow of doubt, he'd found the right woman for the job. 'She's very physical. She adopted this walk – it was almost Charlie Chaplinesque, with her feet barely making little steps. Not overdone, though. The first day, she walked like that and then sat behind the counter [at Retail Rodeo], I went to the producer and said, "She's the character. We've got a movie here."' Arteta went on to compare Jennifer to the actress Mary Pickford, 'who, even though she was glamorous, played regular people, seemed very approachable and had an uncanny knack for physical comedy and for drama'.

But Jennifer remembers the situation differently. On the first day of shooting, she was required to do a scene from the middle of the movie. It was an emotionally tense scene, where Justine decides to get rid of her loved one. Overcome by first-day fear, Jennifer turned to the director and asked if they could start with a different scene. His words would stick with her forever more: 'The way I look at it, you might as well jump chest first into the empty pool.' Thankfully, she jumped and never looked back.

Juggling filming for *The Good Girl* with *Friends*, Jennifer managed to shift effortlessly between comedy and serious drama. It was this duality that made Jennifer such a unique commodity. But the actress shrugged off claims she was doing anything miraculous. 'I don't know. Life can be dramatic and funny all in the same day! So I kind of don't feel that there's a big change. I think you just step into the building, and that other stuff kind of goes out the door.'

Still, she had to confess that both jobs were at completely opposite ends of the spectrum. 'You don't have to deal with that much on *Friends*. You just get to say a good joke and give a good reaction.'

Ultimately, Jennifer enjoyed the light relief of returning to the familiar world of *Friends*. 'Rachel was thankfully such an old comfy pair of shoes. That was almost a relief to go in, it was like having a weekend, going in and laughing, and I can sort of do her. She's easy.' Switching between the two characters wasn't always easy, though. Jennifer described the process as 'exercising muscles that had been asleep for years. I wasn't being allowed to chew other parts of who I really am as an actor, so this role was a big piece to bite off.' Determined to rise to the challenge, Jennifer hired an acting coach to assist with her preparation for the role.

At first, she struggled to lose the famous Rachel mannerisms she'd picked up over the years. 'On our first day of rehearsing, my acting coach said, "Sit on your hands,"' Jennifer said, referring to her famous habit of gesticulating wildly. 'You don't realise you do these things. No wonder everybody says, "She's Rachel, she's Rachel, she's Rachel."' In a bid to solve her 'bad acting habit', she even went to the length of putting 3lb weights on her arms and legs. And in an attempt to distance herself from the 'walking hairstyle' tag, she also agreed not to wash her hair.

Her on-screen love interest, Jake Gyllenhaal, however, was impressed by the ease with which Jennifer moved between light and dark material. 'In this movie, the woman has the power, not the men. You follow this character through the maze, and you should hate her. But, because of the charisma that Jennifer brings to it, you somehow love her. Plus, she plays a humble humour. Some humour is full of arrogance, but hers is done with compassion. She's just so... kind. But there's this dark stuff bubbling underneath, this nice, dark stuff.' He also admired her courage in accepting the role. 'Everyone asks if there's, like, a preconceived notion about working with her,' he said. 'With all that hustle and bustle around her because of the position she is in, I think it's powerful for her to take that risk and risk the failure, risk being criticised. Because everyone wants to criticise her and say, like, all she cares about is her hair when really I think she's just a wonderful person.'

Making *The Good Girl* opened Jennifer to whole new avenues of acting. The film also included her first explicit sex scene. Jake Gyllenhaal joked that he had only accepted the role on the basis of that scene! 'It was the first time I had ever been nude on screen,' shuddered Jennifer. 'I was a movie virgin. It was really painless and it lasted about ten minutes. It was awkward, of course. It's never a comfortable thing, even just having a make-out scene with somebody. Unless you're someone who gets off on having people watch you – which I'm certainly not – it's weird having 40 crew members look at you in such an intimate situation. We had a chastity pillow in between us and our underwear on. We were as naked as we had to be, but not totally naked. Also, since I don't watch myself when this is happening in my real life, I found myself asking, "What do we do now?" Fortunately, Jake was as nervous as I was. Finally, you just go for it. I couldn't ask for a better, sweeter person to be de-virginised on film with.'

The night before Jennifer was due to record the scene, she lay in bed fretting. Brad reassured her everything would be OK. 'Just be nice to the guy,' he joked. 'He's only a kid!'

But, overall, Jennifer didn't have a problem with stripping off for the camera. 'I think, if they're not gratuitous and they serve the story, loves scenes can be beautiful. I just don't like them when they're unnecessary.'

When *The Good Girl* finally wrapped, Jennifer was exhausted. Working so many long hours had finally taken its toll. 'It was almost utter exhaustion. I think that's why I cried a lot on the set... I would never do it again,' she winced. 'Truly. It's not worth it. My sanity and my private life are too important to me.' But, once the film was complete, Jennifer was glad she'd put in the effort. She even managed to watch the final cut all the way through without cringing. 'I don't usually have an easy time of watching anything I've done. In *The Good Girl*, it was a good sign to me that I was able to make it through without cringing. I'm proud of it,' she grinned, adding with a wry smile, 'and it didn't bother me seeing my relaxed-seat jeans at all!'

Brad agreed this was Jennifer's best work yet.

Even though it was never a massive commercial success (the film grossed a respectable £8 million in America, while *Picture Perfect* had pulled in almost twice that amount), *The Good Girl* did open up 'whole new horizons' for Jennifer. Critics praised the actress for her performance. Some even predicted an Oscar nomination, and in one online poll 33 per cent of voters said she should have been nominated for best actress. Jennifer was overwhelmed. 'I knew the part was a good choice, but I don't think anybody ever anticipated this response.' But she was relieved. 'It was almost like my Sally Field moment: "Ooooh, they do like me!" But I remember thinking, OK, now don't get comfortable. You're going to have to work really hard on the next one. This could be it.'

But one thing did strike Jennifer: why had it taken critics this long to realise she was capable of more than raising a smile? 'The weird thing about *The Good Girl* was that suddenly all these people were like, "Wow, look what you can do!" Like I've been doing shitty work for the last nine years or something. Suddenly they're like, "Hey, she's really an actress," as if I were just some bullshit comedienne before.'

As it turned out, she wouldn't have to wait long for the recognition she rightly deserved. In 2002, Jennifer won an Emmy as Outstanding Comedy Actress. In the same year, *Friends* bagged an award for Outstanding Comedy Series and Brad even received a nomination for Outstanding Guest Actor for his appearance in the Thanksgiving Day episode. Ironically, at the time the nominations were announced, the couple were both fast asleep. Jennifer also went on to win a Golden Globe for her work on *Friends* and in 2003 *Forbes* magazine named her the most powerful star on the planet in 2003 in its annual 'Celebrity 100' list. According to their reports, she made $35 million in 2002. 'I don't think anything blossomed in her this year that wasn't already there,' Brad observed. 'It just seems like the rest of the world is waking up to what has been there all along.'

The tides were certainly turning for Jennifer. At last, she seemed to be making headway as a serious actress. It was at the peak of her success that Jennifer decided it was time for a break. 'I want to start my family,' she revealed. 'The best thing to come out of this year is, I took a tiny step forward in allowing myself to continue... I started out wanting to succeed and to prove that I could be an independent working woman. Now I'm seeing the bigger picture, realising that family and enjoying your life are more important than the next role.' But a prolonged break could only mean one thing; Jennifer was ready to quit *Friends*. 'In my mind, I'm done,' she confessed.

Chapter 12

The One Where *Friends* Ends

Since *Friends* first aired in 1994, the show had been nominated for an incredible 44 Emmys and many other awards. It had become one of the most successful TV shows of all time. But both Jennifer and the gang felt they'd reached the end of the road. It was better to quit now while they were miles ahead. 'We want to bow out gracefully. It's going to rip my heart out, but change, when it's necessary, is always a good thing. And there's a big change coming.' It was a tough decision to make. 'It's been like a family, a wonderful dysfunctional family,' she said. 'We grew up together, got married, had babies, had addictions but I think it's done. It's been nine years and I don't know where else it could go.'

Fans were urged to 'cherish every episode' of season nine. But, behind the scenes, producers were desperately trying to cajole the cast into recording a tenth series.

Jennifer appeared to be the main stumbling block. It was unlikely she could commit to an entire 24 episodes and eventually the producers reached a compromise, agreeing on a shorter series of 18 episodes. But Jennifer denied she had been the main spanner in the works. 'It's not complete bullshit, but everybody had an issue. People wanted different things, and doing a shorter season was the compromise. I really wanted to go out on top. And I also felt a little bit like we'd played it out and I didn't know what more we could do, but, sure enough, that's not the case. Thank God we went another year because if we ended last year you would have found me up in a tree somewhere screaming things at people: "I am Rachel!"'

Jennifer found herself in a difficult situation. She was torn between loyalty to her husband and loyalty to the show. 'I had mixed feelings about *Friends* finishing,' she said. 'I wanted to spend more time with Brad and get on with the rest of my life but, on the other hand, I felt a kind of loyalty to the show and didn't want to let everyone else down. That's why we all agreed to do another series just so long as it was a little shorter.'

With a deal firmly in place, only one question now remained – how would the series end? It was the Ross-Rachel-Joey love triangle that had most viewers hooked. Joey and Rachel had become an item after kissing in Barbados. Having treated Rachel like his little sister for much of the series, Matt LeBlanc found some of the scenes difficult to film. 'My instinct was to feel inappropriate.' In fact, most of the cast felt uncomfortable with the idea of Rachel and Joey becoming an item. 'It's one of those storylines where everyone was going leery,' he squirmed. But thankfully the writers managed to 'craft it in a way that is really very clever'.

'Obviously, when Ross finds out about Joey and Rachel, it'll probably be traumatic but handled in a funny way,' said David Schwimmer. 'It's not going to be high drama.' Of course, he hoped Rachel would end up with Ross. 'They're destined to be together. To quote Phoebe Buffay, "They're each other's lobster, whether they know it or not."' But the producers gave the cast very little indication of how the show would end. 'The writers only know about six episodes in advance what's going to happen. The awkward thing is we just never know and people don't believe us.'

With the clock ticking, the world was gripped by a *Friends* frenzy. Oprah Winfrey even recorded a special tribute show with the cast. It was during filming that the reality finally dawned on Jennifer. This was really it. 'I, unfortunately, am one of those blithering idiots who cried on *Oprah*,' winced Jennifer. 'I couldn't stop myself. I really wish I hadn't, but it was this reality check. We've all been in sort of a state of denial about the ending of *Friends* and this kind of made it real. The way she was talking about, "What will you miss? And what are you going to be like the last week? And what do you all think of each other?" And, I mean, we were all like, "Holy shit."' Jennifer's tears quickly set the other cast members off and even Oprah became a little misty-eyed. 'It was just something that took us by surprise,' shrugged Jennifer.

Afterwards, the cast members joked they might have to sedate each other when the series finally wrapped.

As filming for the last show approached, Jennifer reflected on her experiences over the past decade. 'I feel blessed. Complete. Fulfilled. I've been part of something that has brought joy into people's homes, which is a selfishly wonderful feeling. I love not knowing what's going to happen.' She had been just 24 when she signed up to do the series. Now she was 34. 'I've never had a work commitment that lasted this long,' she said, still astounded by the thought. 'I know my bank account has changed, but otherwise I'm the same person I was when I started. I loved *Friends* so much and no other job will compare to it. It's hard. It's ten years of my life working with the most incredible people. It's weird that *Friends* is ending. It doesn't seem like it needs to end, but it does.' From now on, she would cherish every last moment, every last joke and every last hand gesture. 'Even the mundane has meaning. It's silly, but reading my lines as Rachel has deeper significance these days. That's something I've done forever and now I savour it.'

The thought was terrifying, but deep down Jennifer was desperate for the show to end. It was definitely time for Jennifer Aniston to wave goodbye to Rachel Green.

Eager to ensure their last days would be some of their best, Brad booked six suites for Jennifer and her co-stars at the five-star Bellagio in Las Vegas. During the filming of *Ocean's Eleven* he had stayed at the same venue.

When the time came to record the 236th and final episode of *Friends*, a wave of emotion swept through the set.

'We've been on the verge of tears a lot,' confessed Matt LeBlanc. 'This is a gig that changed all of our lives. There will be life after *Friends*, but it's very sad.'

David Schwimmer was also struggling to deal with the inevitable end. 'We're trying not to talk about it.' If someone does get upset, 'the other five try to cheer them up'.

Driving into the Warner Brothers parking lot for the final time, Jennifer felt utterly dazed. 'I felt on the verge of something new and exciting, but I was also experiencing a huge void and deep pain. I was like Bambi, not knowing how to stand up. We're all out of our bodies on the set.'

Jennifer described *Friends* as 'the greatest experience of her life... I probably won't have an experience like that ever again.' Straight after filming, Jennifer drove to a nearby spa to chill out with a seaweed wrap. 'I totally needed it!' Rather than dive into a new project, she opted for a week of relaxation. 'I made a conscious decision not to do anything,' she said. 'I didn't want to be in denial and have it bite me in the butt four months later. I didn't want to go, "Where am I? Who am I?"'

But one thing Jennifer would never do was lose touch with the real friends she'd made on set. She was regularly in contact with all the cast members, particularly Courteney Cox who was one of her best friends. Jennifer was also godmother to Courteney's little girl. 'That bond we all had together – it wasn't phoney; that was real, and it's forever.'

Although Jennifer had no great desire to pursue more TV work at the present, she would happily lend her services to Matt LeBlanc's *Friends* spin-off *Joey*. 'If I was asked to do a spot in it for him, of course I would. I'd do anything for him. I really hope they let Rachel do cameos. Rachel is Joey's friend, so it would be silly if she didn't pop in from time to time.' But Jennifer had no plans to embark on a spin-off series of her own. 'I loved *Friends* so much. I don't know how you could follow that act. It would be silly to say never go back to television, but I feel I've had 15 years doing it and it's time for a change.'

For now, she simply had to focus on her future, which – at this point – was looking good. 'You can't stay in that comfort zone forever. You've got to move it and switch it up and see what happens,' she declared. 'I want to do a lot of things. I want to travel. There's a lot of the world I'd like to see.' Soon, Brad would be filming *Ocean's Twelve* in Rome and Jennifer was already planning a visit.

Closer to home, she was also looking forward to settling into domestic life. Having ditched take-outs, she was learning to cook. 'I made pizza a couple of weeks ago from scratch,' she said. 'I had a kind of Lucy Ethel moment, flour all over me.'

Not once did she worry about disappearing into obscurity. 'You know, if I fade out that quickly, I shouldn't be in this business to begin with. I've just decided that I refuse to be a workaholic. When I do work, I love it and do it as hard as I can. I'm still not over just how lucky I am to have had the jobs I've gotten. As actors, we get to play house and pretend and make people feel good. I mean, I would have been OK with just being a waitress who goes on auditions on the side, you know? So, everything beyond that is just a nice cherry on top.'

The main focus for Jennifer's attentions, however, was to start a family. Now aged 35, her biological clock was ticking. 'Someone will tell me when it's not OK to wear a midriff, right?' she mocked in reference to her age. She did, however, find reassurance in the modern maxim that '40 was the new 30'. 'And don't we have Demi Moore to thank for that? It's almost too much to even take, she's so gorgeous.' In the hope of conceiving without complication, Jennifer had already started taking folic acid. 'We're absolutely in the process of having a baby. It's where we're headed.' She had never planned to have children while *Friends* was still rolling, but now Jennifer was ready to start a new chapter.

Unfortunately, however, limiting her workload was far harder than Jennifer had initially anticipated. Her agents were still swamped by film offers and it was difficult not to be tempted. Eager to settle down, Brad was growing impatient. 'I keep saying, "Jen, when are we going to have babies?" and she says, "Soon,"' he complained in one magazine interview. 'We've been having disagreements about starting our family for years now.'

It didn't help matters that Matt LeBlanc's wife Melissa had recently given birth. 'We sent them baby presents,' said Jennifer. 'I've met her and she's gorgeous. I want to hold her and cuddle her and smell her.' She insisted it wouldn't be long before she and Brad were joining the ranks of parenthood. 'I am elated for them. Now we are making our own plans. We want one.'

Ultimately, these proved to be empty promises. Jennifer couldn't resist taking on more film projects. 'No really, I haven't been busy aside from a little bit of acting and a few things I'm working on for Plan B. Otherwise, I've honestly been really careful to make an effort to stop and smell the roses. With all of the rain we've had lately in LA, there has been a bunch of 'em.'

But who was she kidding? Although she was now free to pick and choose what she did with her time, Jennifer found it impossible to sit around twiddling her thumbs.

Prior to *Friends* finishing, she'd already managed to squeeze in an extra job starring alongside funnyman Jim Carrey in *Bruce Almighty*. Arguably taking a creative step down from *The Good Girl*, Jennifer would once again play the love interest. Jennifer had no qualms about the fact. 'Hopefully if I do the job right, they'll ride with the story.' She wasted no time in accepting the project. 'It just happened really fast. It was a very speedy process, it came about and I said sure.' The script turned out to be a real hit and the film grossed over $200 million in the US alone. 'It's been so much fun working with him,' Jennifer said of Jim Carrey. 'My bones ached from laughing. He's a great physical comedian.' But she went on to qualify that it was his off-camera antics that amused her more. 'When you're doing the scenes, you're watching him go from zero to 60 and you're seeing this whole process. He's funny. You can't help but think he's funny all the time. But he's not "on" all the time, which is great, because that gets exhausting.'

It was in one of Jim Carrey's uncharacteristic moments

of seriousness, however, that he came to save Jennifer's life. High winds caused a crane to topple over on set and he swiftly pushed Jennifer out of its path. He reversed any good work much later in filming when he injured Jennifer during an energetic bedroom scene. 'He just grabbed me, lifted me up and threw me on to the bed. It was like a wrestling throw. I've never been so bruised in my life as I have been working with Jim Carrey,' complained Jennifer. 'I was black and blue.'

Once again, Jennifer confirmed she had A-list Hollywood potential. The cast and crew were suitably impressed by her capabilities. 'Jennifer just has "it",' said the director Tom Shadyac. 'If you look at the handful of A-list actors that exist in Hollywood, you realise that the thing they all share, in addition to being beautiful and talented, is this amazing relatability. When you watch Jennifer, she manages to amaze you and make you feel like she might be your next-door neighbour at the same time, which, when you consider how much money she makes and who she's married to, is pretty incredible.'

Not wishing to waste any time, Jennifer quickly followed suit with another comedy. In *Along Came Polly*, she would star opposite Ben Stiller. She took the part because she 'laughed her head off' when she read the script. But writer John Hamburg insisted the role was still a far cry from Rachel Green. 'It's a pretty big departure for her,' he said. 'She plays this wild woman who draws Ben Stiller out of his shell – someone who's very loose, which is not the way Rachel is at all. I mean, I'm not asking Jennifer to wear a prosthetic nose or anything, but it's very different, and she's very conscious of that. I remember when she first came on the set, she said, "If you feel like I start doing a Rachel thing, just tell me, OK?"'

As it turned out, Jennifer chose to base the character on a friend of hers. 'Polly is based on a girlfriend of mine,' she explained. 'I imitated her and made fun of her, so it was easy. She loved it.'

In preparation for the role, Jennifer was forced to learn a new skill – salsa dancing. 'I was supposed to be a really good salsa dancer in the movie,' she explained. 'I took two classes and I was supposed to take more, but I didn't. It was good. Thank God we got that. We had two days in New York shooting and then the next bit for me was all of the salsa dancing. It was five days straight. My feet looked like raw meat! It was just disgusting. I don't know how those dancers do it, but it was so much fun.' As it turned out, Jennifer broke her toe just six days later. 'I stubbed it on an ottoman,' she fumed. 'It was so stupid. So thank God we took care of all of that stuff. I limped through the rest of the movie.'

That wasn't the only on-set accident. Ben also had an unfortunate incident with a ferret cast in the movie. 'I wasn't a big fan of the ferret,' complained Jennifer. 'It's not the warmest and cuddliest. It bit Ben. I hope I pretended as though I really liked it, but it's just a big rat at the end of the day!'

Fortunately, working with Ben Stiller proved to be a much more pleasurable experience. 'You know when you are listening to jazz and they are just all over the place and it is unexpected? That is sort of like Ben. A riff sure! Ben does things that you sort of don't expect. Like a line, or you hear it or you read it on the page and you know the scene, you can sort of anticipate what will be happening and that just never happens with him. There is never a moment when you feel he is playing comedy. That's what I hate about a lot of comedies, when you're hitting a line or making it funny. Ben just pulls it right out.'

Along Came Polly was released in film theatres a few months before *Friends* ended. It grossed $32 million in its US opening weekend alone and was a number-one box-office smash. Jennifer was stalked by paparazzi. Even Ben Stiller, a bona fide Hollywood A-lister, couldn't believe the amount of attention she received. He recalled an incident during a press junket in Paris. 'With Jen, you can't go anywhere without 20 guys on motorcycles following,' he said. One day she cleverly rented a boat to take Stiller and friends up the Seine to a secret pier. 'These insane photographers are off their bikes, running to catch the boat, and are left screaming on the dock like something out of *Les Misérables*.'

By all accounts, Jennifer was close to achieving the big-time status she'd always desired. With the ghost of Rachel Green laid peacefully to rest, whole new horizons were opening up for the actress. Thanks to credible films like *The Good Girl*, Jennifer had demonstrated herself to be much more than a walking haircut. To an outside observer, Jennifer Aniston was the luckiest lady alive. But, behind the scenes, cracks were starting to show. The work/life balance Jennifer had prided herself upon was starting to buckle under the strain. With so many new projects on the go, her personal life inevitably took a back seat. Once again, the family life she'd promised Brad had slipped down the ladder of priorities. Just one more project, Jennifer thought to herself, and then she'd take a break. But any decisions about her future were soon cruelly snatched from Jennifer's control. Her dreams of starting a family would be shattered. As Jennifer prepared to embark on a new chapter, little did she know it would involve one of the most devastating plot lines of her entire life.

Chapter 13

Love Don't Live Here Anymore

They say absence makes the heart grow fonder, but having spent the past few months apart Brad and Jennifer were inclined to disagree. More often than not, the couple found themselves trying to conduct a relationship from opposite ends of the globe. Self-confessed 'phone junkies', telecommunication became their only form of contact. Sick and tired of the separation, niggling problems started to emerge. The tabloids were filled with reports that dark clouds had settled over the Aniston-Pitt stable. As the pressures of work continued to mount, it appeared Hollywood's golden couple were starting to lose their sheen.

The major bone of contention appeared to centre around Jennifer's reluctance to give up work and have children. According to rumours, Brad was growing increasingly impatient with his ambitious wife. Despite reports the couple were seeking to buy a $3 million home in London, their future together seemed dangerously unsettled. Several ambiguous comments made by the couple in interviews only seemed to fuel gossip further. 'There is so much pressure from day one to be with someone forever, and I'm not sure if it really is in our nature to be with someone for the rest of our lives,' Brad told *Vanity Fair*.

Meanwhile, Jennifer revealed a degree of marital uncertainty in an interview with *W* magazine. 'Is he the love of my life? I think you're always kind of wondering.'

Whereas once Brad and Jennifer had formed a formidable team, gradually they were drifting apart. Once a pillar of support, Jennifer could rely less and less on her husband. Finishing *Friends* was a difficult and traumatic time for Jennifer. 'That was really painful,' she shuddered. 'It was a family and I don't do great with families splitting up. It was hard to have such a wonderful constant in your life, a place to go every day, and then all of a sudden it's not there.' But, when Jennifer needed Brad most, he was nowhere to be seen. 'He just wasn't there for me,' she complained. To everyone's amazement, he didn't even turn up to the final taping of *Friends*. 'He was working,' Jennifer half-heartedly protested in his defence.

The final straw came in December 2004 when Jennifer showed up to the opening of *Ocean's Twelve* without her wedding ring (although it would later appear in subsequent photos).

By now, reports that a split was on the cards were rife in the papers. Seeking some time alone, Brad and Jennifer retreated to the Caribbean island of Anguila for a New Year's break. Although travelling with their friends Courteney Cox and David Arquette, they used the occasion as an opportunity to iron out their differences. Photographs of the couple strolling hand in hand along the beach were splashed across the tabloids. It appeared Brad and Jennifer had successfully steered their marriage back on track. Fans worldwide breathed a sigh of relief.

In fact, quite the opposite was true. It was later reported that Brad had returned home early to watch a football match in LA. Then, on 7 January 2005, Brad and Jennifer dropped a bombshell that would rock the celebrity world. After seven years together and four and a half years of happy marriage, the couple had agreed to call it quits and go their separate ways.

Brad's publicist issued a joint statement outlining their course of action. 'For those who follow these sorts of things, we would like to explain that our separation is not the result of any speculation reported by the tabloid media – this decision is the result of much thoughtful consideration. We happily remain committed and caring friends with great love and admiration for one another. We ask in advance for your kindness and sensitivity in the coming months.'

Two months later, Jennifer filed for divorce.

Speculation was rife in the media as to what had really caused the split. Only months previously, Brad and Jennifer had gushed about their marriage to the press. They were the unshakable couple, the love that must just defy Hollywood tradition and last forever. So what had gone wrong? Was Jennifer's reluctance to start a family really the root cause of the split? 'That was one version of events,' Brad told one magazine, 'and total bullshit, by the way.' But he refused to give any further details. 'It's not one thing,' he pleaded. 'It's so complex and multifaceted.'

Instead, he remained philosophical about the whole episode. In spite of all that had happened, he would never regret his time with Jennifer. Those had been some of the happiest years of his life. 'I know that, if a marriage doesn't fit a certain idea, it's looked upon as a failure,' he says. 'But I see mine as a total success. My God, man, Jen is such an influence on my life. We made it for seven years – that's five years more than I made it with anyone else… We really put everything on the table. We didn't hide who we were or what we wanted in any way. I think it was bold on our parts and really successful.

'Anything worth anything is a beast,' he shrugged. 'The thing I don't understand is looking at this as a failure. It's talked about like it failed, I guess because it wasn't flawless. Me, I embrace the messiness of life. I find it so beautiful, actually.' In his opinion, a successful marriage need not necessarily last forever. 'I still really believe in it. I'm sure there are some dark nights coming, but that's the deal – that's part of it. A friend of mine wrote to me, "Sometimes love changes shape." And I just thought, That's so well put.'

Jennifer, however, found the break-up much tougher to deal with. Although in public she was a picture of grace and reserve, in private the actress was an emotional wreck. Unable to deal with the constant reminders of

Brad, she moved out of their marital home and took up temporary residence with her gay hairdresser Chris McMillan (responsible for the famous Rachel haircut and styling for her wedding day). 'She couldn't face going back to the house shared with Brad,' reported a friend. 'She found the idea too upsetting. Chris has been a great shoulder to cry on for her over the years and he's there for her now.'

While Jennifer remained admirably silent, others couldn't wait to offer their opinion on why the marriage had failed. Brad's ex-fiancée Gwyneth Paltrow suggested the couple had perhaps been too open with their relationship. While they were willing to share their happiness when the marriage was in good shape, now they were paying the inevitable price.

To some extent, Jennifer would agree. 'You know, she's right. She's absolutely correct. I feel like there is a graveyard of celebrity couples who now have learned their lesson. You know, at the time you go, "Celebrate it – we're in love, and let's talk, and who cares?" Part of that's true. It kind of became a bizarre feeding frenzy for a period there. It just got a little out of control, that's all. So you learn those lessons. It's just about learning what to keep sacred.'

Admittedly, however, the media hadn't help. Their portrayal of Jennifer and Brad as the picture-perfect couple was far from realistic.

More than anything, Jennifer was extremely offended by the sensationalist stories claiming she was unwilling to give Brad a child. 'A man divorcing would never be accused of choosing career over children,' she fumed. 'That really pissed me off. I've never in my life said I didn't want to have children. I did, I do and I will! The women that inspire me are the ones who have careers and children; why would I want to limit myself? I've always wanted to have children, and I would never give up that experience for a career. I want to have it all.'

One unnamed mutual friend even went on to suggest that Brad had in fact been the stumbling block to starting a family. 'When Brad and Jen were in the marriage, having a baby was not his priority – ever. It was an abstract desire for him, whereas for Jen it was much more immediate. So is there a part of Brad that's diabolical? Did he think, I need to get out of this marriage, but I want to come out smelling like a rose, so I'm going to let Jen be cast as the ultra-feminist and I'm going to get cast as the poor husband who couldn't get a baby and so had to move on?'

With every newspaper report, the plot thickened. Perhaps Brad and Jennifer's break-up wasn't quite as amicable as everyone had imagined. But exactly what diabolical skeletons was Brad hiding in his closet? Slowly another explanation started to emerge. A third party must be involved.

Towards the end of their marriage, Brad had been working on a new film *Mr & Mrs Smith*. His co-star was notorious man-eater and sex siren Angelina Jolie. Twice divorced, Angelina had a scandalous past involving rumours of bisexuality, brotherly incest and heroin. Both she and her estranged husband Billy Bob Thornton had a reputation for bizarre sexual activities and she even carried a vial of his blood around her neck. In the past, Angelina had confessed to a habit of falling for her leading men. 'I have always developed deep ties with actors who have played alongside me. I always fall in love,' she said.

Her statement only served to fan the flames of tabloid gossip. Could Brad have done the unthinkable and left America's sweetheart for another woman?

Brad preferred not to comment. When asked whether Angelina had contributed to the breakdown of his marriage, he replied, 'And it's pretty much still going that way, is what I hear.' Instead, he criticised the media machine for causing unnecessary upset. 'Jen and I have felt pretty impervious to it all. We have not seen a thing, so that we can carry on in this new incarnation with the love we still have for each other. My attitude was, say what you want, we're not playing.' As far as he was concerned, the reasons behind the split were strictly between himself and Jennifer. 'The only thing to figure out is between Jen and I. And there's a beauty in that. There's a beauty in our coming together, there's a beauty in our time together, and there's a beauty in this, for us. I'm actually really proud of us. We've done it another way – we've done it our way, and I love her for that. We've kept the love we have for each other.'

Dealing with the media frenzy had become unbearable and reduced Brad to a near fugitive. It was a problem he and Jennifer had battled throughout their relationship. 'Outside our house, mine and Jen's, we had teams there every day. You'd have one team of three cars, a secondary team of three cars. And you'd drag 'em across town, but some days you just don't want to play.' Although caught in the media maelstrom himself, Brad was more concerned for the safety of his estranged wife. 'They're really nasty out here. I mean, some of the things they've said during my and Jen's split – things that are just deliberately said to get a rise out of her, just truly cruel – make me want to punch their lights out. And more toward Jen than me, which made me even more mad, because Jen's an easier target. Grown men saying awful despicable things. Things that a normal father or husband or brother would go and kill them for... I don't expect anyone to have any sympathy, but they're horrendous, man, and I take great pride in being their nemesis. There's no respect. It's a blood sport: They hate us and we hate them.'

It was a touching response, but not everyone was so easily convinced of Brad's innocence. Courteney Cox was reportedly incensed by his behaviour and Brad would later confess to receiving an angry phone message from his mother. 'I'm disappointed in you, I'm angry with you, but whatever you do I'll always love you,' he quoted her as saying. Shrugging, he confessed, 'All my bitches are mad at me right now.' But he declined to elaborate.

Residing nowhere in particular, he had been hotel hopping since splitting with Jennifer. Recently, he'd purchased a new place near the beach, which he described simply as 'something I'm squatting in right now'.

As media speculation raged, both Brad and Jennifer remained tight-lipped on the topic. But, much to

Jennifer's embarrassment, Brad refused to keep a low profile. He and Angelina were photographed in various exotic locations. Often Brad would be seen playing and lovingly caring for Angelina's adopted Cambodian son Maddox. In April, pictures emerged of the couple frolicking on the beach with Maddox at a romantic resort in Africa. The pair also embarked on several energetic trips to Third World countries, fulfilling Angelina's responsibilities as a goodwill ambassador for the United Nations. In July, Brad accompanied Angelina to Ethiopia, where she adopted her second child Zahara Marley, an AIDS orphan.

Speaking about the experience, Brad told reporters, 'I'm telling you, you just wanna take 'em [the orphans] up in your arms and take as many with you as you can.' So would he be following in Angelina's footsteps? 'I don't know how I can't adopt now, seeing what I've seen. Yeah, it makes all the sense in the world to me. I'm going back in a couple of weeks. There's some kids I want to visit; it's as much for me as them.'

Although it now appeared obvious he and Angelina were enjoying more than just a platonic relationship, Brad refused to divulge any details. Speaking about Angelina's influence on his life, he merely said, 'I certainly respect what she's done, but many people have been working to alleviate poverty and AIDS, Bono especially – and, yeah, her as well. And a host of others. She contributes staggering amounts of money – staggering amounts. In fact, she probably makes money so she can give more away. That seems to be more her concern than films.'

Angelina refused to shed any further light. She merely described Brad as 'a great actor... a very genuine person. Anybody who's met him would know that. You can read him, and you can feel that there's something open and approachable and interesting. And he's just very real. Whether cameras are rolling or not, he doesn't change. He's very solid. I think you know you can count on him.'

As for her personal life, it was no one's business but her own. 'People want an answer about what's happening in my life and my family, but I need to know what's happening first,' she explained. 'And I don't plan to discuss it before then. It's not about censoring myself. It's that there's nothing to say until I know that there's something to say.' But she did hint that love was no longer enough to forge a lasting union. 'Basically, I think there should be a reason for you to be a unit. Not just to be happy, but to actually accomplish and change, and take on the things you want to take on in this life.'

When Brad applied for legal adoption of Angelina's children in December 2005, however, all rumours were finally confirmed. Still the couple refrained from comment. Instead, Brad's publicist Cindy Guagenti issued a statement. 'We are confirming that Brad Pitt is in the process of becoming the adoptive father of both children,' she told the press.

Once the legal process was completed, both children were given the surnames Jolie-Pitt. But, contrary to rumour, Brad and Angelina had no plans to tie the knot. Speaking about whether he would eventually remarry, Brad said, 'I can't even think that way, trying to decipher what this new incarnation is, and still feeling the aroma of what was, and my Jen, and what it's gonna be. I'm not ready to think that way yet, and I think she'd say the same... I'm not worried that it's not gonna happen. I'll make it happen. You go make the things that you want.'

While Brad's concern for his ex-wife was certainly noble, his actions had hurt her deeply. In private, she recoiled in humiliation, but in front of the cameras she refused to give anything away. Back in September 2005, she chose to break her silence with an extremely frank interview in US magazine *Vanity Fair*. In the past, Jennifer had expressed infidelity as one of her greatest fears. 'I've never been cheated on,' she told *Marie Claire* in 1996. 'But it's one of my biggest fears – being cheated on or left. I guess that comes from watching my mom deal with it.'

With the news Brad had shacked up with another woman, Jennifer was forced to face one of her greatest fears. 'It was extremely hurtful to Jen that he was seen with another woman so quickly after they were separated,' said close friend Andrea Bendewald.

At the time of the split, Brad insisted he hadn't slept with Angelina. Of course, there was an attraction, but Jennifer accepted nothing untoward had taken place. 'She's not suggesting she didn't know there was an enchantment, and a friendship,' said friend Kristin Hahn. 'But Brad was saying, "This is not about another woman."'

Courteney Cox also gave Brad the benefit of doubt. 'I don't think he started an affair with her physically, but I think he was attracted to her. There was a connection and he was honest about that with Jen. Most of the time, when people are attracted to other people, they don't tell. At least he was honest about it. It was an attraction that he fought for a period of time.'

Discussing the separation statement she and Brad had carefully penned together, Jennifer told *Vanity Fair*, 'What we said was true... as far as I knew. We wrote it together, very consciously, and felt very good about it. We exited this relationship as beautifully as we entered it.'

Ultimately, however, Jennifer felt hurt and betrayed by the speed with which Brad had jumped into a full-blown relationship with Angelina. Casting her mind back over events, she painstakingly searched for clues that might indicate the pair had been having an affair.

She recalled meeting Angelina only once. 'It was on the lot of *Friends*,' she recounted. 'I pulled over and introduced myself.' Jennifer went on to gush about how excited Brad was to be working with the actress. 'I hope you guys have a really good time,' she wished her, with genuine sincerity. Now those same words stung with bitter irony.

For the sake of her own sanity, however, Jennifer chose to believe Brad when he insisted Angelina was not the cause of his marital discontent. 'At this point, I wouldn't be surprised by anything,' sighed an emotionally exhausted Jennifer. 'But I would much rather choose to believe him.'

There was only so much Jennifer could take. When a 60-page photo spread featuring Brad and Angelina as an early 1960s-style married couple with kids appeared in *W* magazine, Jennifer was horrified. Entitled 'Domestic Bliss', it went straight for the jugular. Not only was the article humiliating, worse still Brad had orchestrated the entire shoot himself. He even retained the international rights and thus actually profited from it. 'He makes his choices – he can do whatever,' sighed Jennifer. 'We're divorced, and you can see why. I can also see Brad had absolutely no clue why people would be appalled by it. Brad is not mean-spirited; he would never intentionally try to rub something in my face. In hindsight, I can see him going, "Oh, I can see that that was inconsiderate." But I know Brad. Brad would say, "That's art!"'

Courteney Cox agreed that Brad had never intentionally set out to offend Jennifer. 'I don't think he was trying to hurt Jen. He's not malicious or a liar. The *W* thing was his idea, but I don't think he thought that one through, about what it would look like to anyone else.'

Admirably, Jennifer struggled to see the situation from Brad's perspective. Fed up with confrontation in her life, she had no desire to declare an unnecessary war. 'I'm not interested in taking pot shots,' she explained. 'It's not my concern any more. What happened to him after the separation – it's his life now. I've made a conscious effort not to add to the toxicity of this situation. I haven't retaliated. I don't want to be a part of it. I would much rather everyone move on.' But it didn't change the fact she had been incredibly hurt by Brad's flagrant display of disregard. 'There's a sensitivity chip that's missing,' she declared with frustration.

More than anything, Jennifer was determined not to make the same mistakes as her parents. 'I learned by example of what not to do by watching my parents. I watched my mother be very bitter and very angry throughout a divorce and never let it go and waste the whole second half of her life,' claimed Jennifer. 'I thank her for that unconscious sacrifice of what not to do.'

Retreating from the public eye, Jennifer took time to evaluate the past few months. It would have been easy to assume the role of a wronged woman, lashing out at Brad and Angelina for destroying her life. But Jennifer knew life wasn't so black and white. 'It's so easy to blame. That's just a waste of time,' she concluded.

Instead, she would work this one out in private and with dignity. Seeking some time alone, Jennifer set up home in a Malibu bungalow. Filled with white sofas, white flowers and white candles, it was a picture of calm and serenity – a million miles from the tumultuous storm gathering in Jennifer's head.

Jennifer had taken pride in decorating the place. When she arrived, it was a dark and depressing shell. Within days, she had transformed the place into a cosy sanctuary. Asian artefacts were displayed throughout, including stone bowls filled with koi and lotus blossoms and Buddha statues. A haze of exotic incense swirled around the room. 'It's beautiful here; I love it,' she cooed. 'I've always wanted to have a little Malibu beach house, and it feels good. I'm enjoying simplifying things.' Jennifer enjoyed the process of decorating to her own tastes. It was a relief to escape the cold and clinical décor Brad had always favoured. 'Brad and I used to joke that every piece of furniture was either a museum piece of furniture or just uncomfortable,' she laughed.

She described the new house as 'comfortable', 'eclectic' and 'very sexy'. 'I literally had two weeks to redo the place from tiling to ripping out cabinets,' she said, proud of her achievement. In need of a helping hand, she called upon a friend who happened to be a film-set designer. 'They make a set in a day,' Jennifer explained. 'A set designer creates a home. You walk on to all these sets and go, "God, this looks great!" So I called her and said, "Will you help me dress a set? I need to dress a set, but I'm going to live in it." It was the most fun I've ever had. We went shopping for two days.'

For once, she was in full control. With only herself for consideration, she no longer needed to seek Brad's approval. In fact, the only reminder of her estranged husband was a picture of a small Asian boy cuddling an elephant, taken by his favourite photographer Gregory Colbert. 'He definitely had his sense of style, and I definitely have my sense of style, and sometimes they clashed. I wasn't so much into modern.' There were certainly some benefits to be had from single life. 'I can have a comfortable couch!' she smiled.

Often Jennifer would take long contemplative strolls along the beach, the Pacific Ocean rumbling in the background, trying to figure out exactly where her marriage had gone wrong. Sometimes she would sit on the deck outside her house, listening to waves rhythmically lap the shoreline. 'That's quite a backyard, in my opinion,' she would smile. 'Just being able to go to the water's edge and scream,' she continued, pausing to correct herself, 'not too loudly. You don't want people to think that you're crazy, but it can be cathartic.'

Jennifer chose to hide from the world 'in an effort to take care of myself and my heart. I'm trying to hatch a plan where I don't actually have to leave the house, and I think I'm figuring it out. I haven't got it quite down,' she quipped. So far, her longest stretch had been six days. 'I had walks on the beach. I got as much of my reading done as I could. I thought it was great.'

Jennifer used the time to unravel a ball of confused thoughts. She described herself as 'a processor'. At night, she would go to sleep with questions and problems, only to wake with answers and solutions. 'I wake up and I'm like, I have to move the couch, you know? Or I gotta call my mother. Who knows? It could be, I don't know... How am I going to get through the next few months with some dignity and grace?' If she kept an open mind, Jennifer believed she would be more receptive to solutions. 'They say there's a certain time of the night or the morning when you're more open to receiving information – if there is information to be received – if you're one of those New Agers who believe that stuff, which I've been known to do. I love that stuff.'

Having been in an all-consuming relationship for all those years, single life would definitely take some getting used to. Jennifer certainly had her down days. 'I've thrown a little pity party for myself,' she confessed. 'I'm a partnership person and if something happens your instinct is to share it – but you're no longer part of a couple. I definitely miss that. It's sort of like Bambi – like you're trying to learn how to walk. You're a little awkward; you stumble a little bit.'

That said, Jennifer saw her solo mission as a positive

journey. 'I've had lonely moments, but I'm also enjoying being alone. It's uncharted territory, but it's good for me to be a solo person right now. You're forced to rediscover yourself and take it to another level. If you can find a way to see the glass half-full, these are the moments when you learn the most. I've had to reintroduce myself to myself in a way that's different.'

But Jennifer wasn't always alone. The close group of girlfriends she'd had for almost 20 years quickly rallied round. These were no fair-weather friends – they were people who cared for Jennifer's mental health and wellbeing. 'I've got an unbelievable support team, and I'm a tough cookie,' she insisted. 'I have so much love. My female friends – they're my sisters, my partners. They're my everything. It's hard to find a man who can live up to any of them.

'When things happen, the tribe gathers round and lifts you up.' Every week, the 12-strong group would meet up to share problems and seek advice. 'It's free group therapy,' smiled Jennifer. 'We've all moved on with our lives, some of us are married and have had babies, and we are all sort of evolving, and we just keep each other together. I love them, they are my everything. And, if one of us is not doing well, we always have a rally and we kidnap them and take them away. We rescue them!'

She certainly needed assistance, but Jennifer was far from a helpless victim in need of rescue. 'This woman is basically having a root canal without anaesthesia, but she's really trying not to numb the pain or shove it under the rug,' said her friend Kristin Hahn in admiration. 'She's grown so much and she continues to grow on a daily basis, because every time you think, Well, I've dealt with this, there's another hurdle to get over. It's a bit Job-like at the moment.'

Another close pal, Andrea Bendewald, was equally in awe of Jennifer's remarkable resolve. 'She is grieving, but she's taken the high road. She's mourning the death of a marriage, and she's done it very privately. She can have her moments of rage, but she doesn't want to out him, and that keeps her heart clear. She's not bad-mouthing him. She doesn't want to make him the villain and her the victim.'

In search of further enlightenment, Jennifer also embarked on a course of therapy. In the past, she had called on her therapist to assist with family problems and insecurities stemming from childhood. Now it was time to call on her services once again. However, by a cruel twist of fate, Jennifer's trusted therapist had passed away just one month before the split with Brad. 'I will cherish this woman forever. It was very sad because I thought she was a very smart, wise woman and unbelievably helpful to me. So it was devastating.' Still retaining her sense of humour, she didn't fail to miss the irony of the situation. 'When your shrink dies, you just go, "Really? Is this some kind of cosmic joke?" I will never forget that moment. I was like, "Wow. Well. OK. Let's put your money where your mouth is and walk through this." Because, that December, I knew that everything was sort of... coming. And then I was like, "Oh, right. You did retain it. It does work." And you do build strength if you're really committed to the work. But it is, in an odd way, funny. Just as I arrived at the threshold of this grand door. "So, are you in therapy? No, she died." It's very funny. I mean, this is the thing. Isn't it all funny? Thank God, we can have a sense of humour. Good God!'

For a period, Jennifer turned to self-help books. But, after overindulging herself on other people's advice, she realised it was time to trust in her own instincts. 'I've read many self-help books,' she confessed. 'I believe in being an "everythingist". There's always a little thread of some beauty to everything. I love that! But right now I couldn't look at a self-help book if I was dying in the middle of the street and it told me how I didn't have to die in the middle of the street. I couldn't do it. I'm not in that place right now.'

Instead, she channelled her stresses through budokan, a form of karate focusing on spiritual wellbeing and physical fitness. In a bid to regain some calm, she attended classes three times a week. She also enjoyed yoga, an obsession responsible for her new svelte figure.

Over time, Jennifer drew her own conclusions on events of the previous 12 months. Most importantly, she would never let her sadness poison the happiness she had once shared with Brad. Nothing could take that away from her. Marriage, after all, was a journey without any guaranteed destination. 'It's like the ebb and flow of any relationship,' she pondered. 'It's hard; it gets easy; it gets fun again. What's hard to sustain is some ideal that it's perfect. That's ridiculous. What's fantastic about marriage is getting through those ebbs and flows with the same person, and looking across the room and saying, "I'm still here. And I still love you." You re-meet, reconnect. You have marriages within marriages within marriages. That's what I love about marriage. That's what I want in marriage.'

In part, Jennifer blamed a 'disposable society' for the ease with which people were willing to give up on relationships and commitment. Rather than throw in the towel, couples should embrace those moments as 'transformative moments'. 'Most couples draw up divorce papers when they're missing out on an amazing moment of deepening and enlightenment and connection,' she explained.

It saddened her that she and Brad didn't share quite the same view. 'We believe in different things, I guess,' she said glumly. 'You can't force a relationship, even if it is your view of how you'd like it to be conducted. Obviously, two people leave a relationship because there's a different thought pattern happening. My goal is to achieve a very deep, committed relationship. That's what I'm interested in, but it's someone's prerogative to be or not to be in or out of a relationship.'

Nevertheless, Jennifer cherished every minute of her marriage. She would love Brad for the rest of her life. 'I still feel so lucky to have experienced it. I wouldn't know what I know now if I hadn't been married to Brad. I love Brad. I really love him. I will love him for the rest of my life. He's a fantastic man. I don't regret any of it, and I'm not going to beat myself up about it. We spent seven intense years together; we taught each other a lot – about healing, and about fun. We helped each other through a lot and I really value that. It was a beautiful, complicated relationship.'

Essentially, problems had arisen when she and Brad had ceased growing together. It was time for Jennifer to step off this particular ride. That was the hardest thing to accept. 'We both changed,' she sighed. 'We did the best we could.'

Jennifer's pals agreed Jennifer had remained committed to the marriage, but that Brad had reached a point in life where he no longer knew what he wanted. In all the confusion, he felt it was impossible to remain married. After months of trying to persuade him otherwise, Jennifer eventually gave in and let him go. Jennifer had always valued her relationship with Brad as something special, a love that transcended all the usual flimsy Hollywood unions. 'The sad thing, for me, is the way it's been reduced to a Hollywood cliché – or maybe it's just a human cliché.'

In her more upbeat moments, Jennifer viewed the whole experience as a learning curve. Appearing on *The Oprah Winfrey Show*, she opened her heart to the world. Oprah had become a close and trustworthy friend over the years. Jennifer couldn't think of a better medium through which to communicate her story to fans. 'What makes Oprah so special is her commitment to authenticity,' enthused Jennifer. 'She lives her life with no apologies. I think that's why she's unbelievable at giving and she's constantly a student, she's never an authority on anything. I think that's what makes her so accessible and why people love her so much. You never feel dumb, you feel like you're all figuring it out together and she's not above us, she's with us.'

Oprah even went so far as to invite Jennifer and her pals to spend a mini-vacation in her private guesthouse. 'What I felt from your girls was such a bond – it was like you were all sisters. In the morning, I called to see if Jen was all right, and they were all in the same bed! I go, "Those are real friends!" That must have been very helpful to you during trying times.'

But, even miles from her own home, Jennifer enjoyed little respite from the prying paparazzi. 'I've been living in peace all this time,' teased Oprah. 'And then you show up at my house and I've got helicopters going around. How does it make you feel to have your every move tracked like that?'

During the TV interview, Jennifer was extremely candid about her split with Brad. 'Here's one thing I know: the greater your capacity to love, the greater your capacity to feel pain,' she concluded. 'I know for sure that it hurts and yet I love it.' Overall, Jennifer was proud of the woman she was growing into. 'I'm proud of what Brad and I have done for each other. I'm a child of a nasty divorce and, in spite of that, I still saw that love was possible.'

'That's the real lesson that she's teaching everybody,' said friend Shirley MacLaine in an interview. 'She says so in public and certainly in private, "Where is my role in this? How have I contributed to this?" in a very spiritual way instead of blaming. That's a huge step and really hard.'

After much thought and consideration, Jennifer had

reached a point of calm stoicism. 'It's a clichéd thing to say, "Everything happens for a reason",' she explains. 'It's one of those things when you want to punch somebody when you hear it. If I had a dollar for everyone who told me that… But the true story is – yes, it does!'

Exhausted by sadness, Jennifer was ready to move on. 'I am not defined by this relationship,' she complained. 'I wasn't when I was in it and I don't want to be in the aftermath of it. And that's really important to me. I am not defined by the part they're making me play in the triangle. It's maddening to me. Let's let everybody move on and live their lives, and hopefully everybody will be really happy.'

But there was still one further blow in store. In January 2006, news emerged that Angelina was pregnant with Brad's baby. According to reports, Angelina had let slip her secret to a charity aid worker in Santo Domingo in the Dominican Republic. Eventually, news filtered down to Jennifer, but there were conflicting reports as to how exactly she found out. One magazine suggested Jennifer had called Brad's mobile phone, only to find Angelina on the other end. Angelina had no idea who was calling as the number came up as private. Apparently, the girls chatted amicably, before Angelina handed the phone to Brad. Another report alleged Angelina had taken the initiative to contact Jennifer. A final version of events claimed Brad had done the honours. Dignified throughout, Jennifer had wished the couple well, saying she hoped the baby would be healthy and that Angelina's pregnancy would run smoothly. Minutes later, however, she hung up and burst into tears.

The real story remained unclear, but one thing was for certain – Jennifer was heartbroken. Months earlier, her friend Kristin had expressed fears that a situation of this sort might transpire. 'My worst fear is that Jen will have to face them having a baby together soon, because that would be beyond painful,' she warned.

When one journalist even broached the subject, Jennifer physically crumpled, her eyes welling up with tears. The topic was too painful to even discuss.

With the news Brad and Angelina were expecting a child, the media pressure stepped up a gear. Jennifer blamed a public obsession with reality-TV shows. 'This is what I think the problem is: we have such an obsession with reality TV,' she complained. 'What happened to a great half-hour sitcom? It's all *Dancing with the Stars*! Knitting with the Stars! Building a Home with the Stars! Living in the Homes of the Stars! And then ripping people to shreds. Humiliation. Degradation. What is going on?'

There was a time when she and Brad found such shows amusing. Entire programmes had been dedicated to her perfect marriage. Jennifer recalled one particular programme called *It's Good To Be Brad and Jen*. 'It was all about us going to Scotland and Greece and having our matching SUVs and it wasn't my life. I'd never even been to some of these places but even I got sucked in.' Both she and Brad would joke about what a 'great life Brad and Jen must lead'.

Given the current circumstances, however, Jennifer wished the spotlight would shift elsewhere. Defiantly, she refused to even switch on her TV set. 'I don't watch TV any more. Nothing. I have no interest in that *Idol* shit. The world is in such a state with this war and everything else, and it's easier to go and look at the triteness of a celebrity break-up. It's like, Ahhh, relief. It's an escape, like a daytime soap opera.'

For her own peace of mind, it was best if Jennifer remained oblivious to the media storm gathering around her. 'It's been very important for me not to read anything, not to see anything,' she said. 'It's been my saving grace. That stuff is just toxic for me right now. I probably avoided a lot of suffering by not engaging in it, not reading, not watching.'

Desperate for a photo of Jennifer crumbling under pressure, photographers would trail her on a daily basis. One particularly insistent snapper even scaled a nine-foot fence and snuck into Jennifer's house. Fortunately, it was on one of the rare occasions she was out of town. He was chased down the beach by her housekeeper, arrested for burglary and ordered to come no closer than one hundred yards of Jennifer until 2008.

Not everyone in the press was quite so threatening. Many writers championed Jennifer as a heroine and credited the actress for her grace and maturity in dealing with the break-up. 'People have been great,' she admitted. 'There's a lot of respect. I really appreciate it.' Brad and Jennifer's divorce had divided the nation and the press were more than happy to draw up the battle lines. One bright spark even conjured up the idea of screen-printing 'Team Aniston' and 'Team Jolie' T-shirts. According to one Hollywood boutique, 'Team Aniston' T-shirts were outselling 'Team Jolie' T-shirts by a margin of 25 to 1.

In public, strangers would frequently approach Jennifer and offer their condolences. 'I've consoled a lot of weeping, wonderful people. It's quite moving. I've had a Greek woman in an elevator go off in Greek about something. It wasn't very nice but I've had all kinds of the strangest experiences – name it.'

Although Jennifer was flattered by so much support, the last thing she wanted was pity. 'I don't feel like a victim,' she declared. 'I've worked with a therapist for a long time, and her major focus is that you get one day of being a victim – and that's it. Then we take responsibility for our own input. To live in a victim place is pointing a finger at someone else, as if you have no control.'

As far as Jennifer was concerned, both making and breaking a relationship was a joint effort. 'Relationships are two people; everyone is accountable. A lot goes into a relationship coming together and a lot goes into a relationship falling apart.' She went on to quote her therapist: 'Even if it's 98 per cent the other person's fault, it's 2 per cent yours, and that's what we're going to focus on.' After months of soul-searching, Jennifer made one important discovery: 'You can only clean up your side of the street.'

Putting the whole thing into perspective, Jennifer pointed out that her experience was nothing unusual.

Sadly, divorce was now a universal phenomenon. 'There are so many women who are crippled by divorce,' she claimed. 'Crippled by it. Can't walk, and can't wake up again. I felt like there was a little part of it that I could put out there that was not about airing my dirty laundry but was just sort of saying that you can get through something like this and be as happy, if not happier, again.' Besides, worse things were happening in the world. 'Compared to what other people are surviving out there in the world, this is not so bad in the grand scheme of things. Human endurance is unbelievable. Think of what mothers of soldiers have to rise above! Everything's relative.

'I'm not a role model or the poster child for how to do anything... I don't have a particular halo that I'm polishing,' she cautioned. 'This was my first time at this particular picnic.' The compliments bestowed upon her were, at times, difficult to bear. 'It's a very heavy mantle to be wearing.' In fact, Jennifer's silence was as much down to self-preservation. She'd learned from experience that some things should be left unsaid. But it wasn't easy. 'It's so hard, it's almost the impossible – not talking about anything,' she complained. 'I don't abide well to gag orders. I'm a talker. Not like a gossiper, but I'm a sharer of life. I love people who share. I think it's a beautiful trait when people are not micro-managing every corner of their life. But there is a boundary. I've learned my lessons throughout the years on when the line gets crossed and how that can be used against you and can backfire. '

One positive outcome of Jennifer's prolonged period of

reflection was a reconciliation with her estranged mother. Determine to straighten her life out once and for all, Jennifer knew it was time to rebuild bridges. Initially, her approach was tentative. 'We've exchanged messages,' she told friends. 'Our doors are open. We're taking baby steps and it's a good thing.' Looking back, however, Jennifer had no regrets. Excluding her mother from the wedding had been a difficult decision, but it was one Jennifer had been right to make. 'I feel pretty good about the choices I've made,' she concluded. 'The choice of not speaking to Mom for a while – that's ours. Nobody else has to understand it. The same with Brad and myself. I wouldn't change my childhood, I wouldn't change my heartaches, I wouldn't change any of it, because I really love who I am, and I am continuing to become.'

Ultimately, Jennifer was thrilled by the prospect of a reunion with her mother. She took pleasure in the fact that every cloud really did have a silver lining. 'Who knew that this divorce would be the thing to initiate it?' she pondered thoughtfully. 'It's amazing. It's like we get to reintroduce ourselves to each other. I'm just happy she's still here. Parent/child relationships are always so complicated and fraught with all sorts of Louis Vuitton baggage.'

With time and distance, Jennifer saw much of her mother in her own character. Having been through a divorce herself, she had newfound empathy with Nancy's behaviour. 'I can almost guarantee you I am probably a carbon copy of her at this point. It's the thing of "what you resist persists". I hear myself speak and I'm like, "Oh, my God, I am Nancy. I'm Nancy!" I'm the evolved Nancy that had the opportunities and awareness that we have today. And I'm not saying there weren't issues that took place that led to this. But I really see now whether I was judging her on how she handled her separation or her situation. They didn't have the advantages that we have with therapy, with self-help books.'

Finally, the dark cloud hanging over Jennifer's life appeared to be lifting. 'This year has been the best and the worst of times,' she mused. But the healing process was beginning to take effect. Jennifer appreciated the time out she'd allowed herself. 'I didn't have to do anything I didn't want to last year. I didn't have to go out into the world at all.' Now she was ready to face the music. Of course, she was apprehensive. 'I am a little bit nervous about the future, but I definitely feel ready to move on. My pain was real, but I'll tell you what: there's such a freedom in a weird way; you can just say, "Here I am – this is it."'

For the first time, she was starting to accept life after Brad. 'This doesn't kill you. You move on. You can't let the devastation of a divorce take over and win – let it make you this bitter, closed-off, angry, sceptical person. Then you're falling victim to it. You don't want to shut your heart down. You don't want to feel that, when a marriage ends, your life is over.'

During her time away, she had also learned to embrace solitude. 'Before, I never had the chance. I was always with friends and roommates. If I had a night off, I thought, I don't want to be by myself. Now, getting older, I crave it. I even travel alone, take a week and go by myself to a hotel on a beach. Lying out in the sun is a year-round thing. Even during winter in LA, I'm out there. And in hotel rooms I can completely entertain myself: read, watch movies, go to the spa, take a walk, just close my eyes and do nothing. Of course, I get a little lonely once in a while, but nothing's wrong with that. What's important is being able to sit with yourself.'

Waving goodbye to one part of her life, she was ready for a new adventure. 'There are really powerful things that happen out of this sort of loss. That's the stuff that life is made of. If you don't have appreciation for it – if you haven't sat in the dark depths of sadness and pain – you can't appreciate feeling good. It's like when you're really sick and all of a sudden you have that day when you wake up and finally feel great. You're like a kid in a candy store. I can't believe how great I feel! At the end of the day, it's just yourself, your own work, your own resilience, and your faith in yourself. I really believe that everything is meant to be. You can't ask, "Why is this happening to me?" It's happening to you! Life's tough. Get a helmet.'

These days, Jennifer could 'sleep better, function better and do her job better'. She took great pleasure in newfound hobbies. 'I love to be with my friends. I love being in my home, cooking, going out to dinner. I like to watch movies, I like to take hikes and I like to take the car and go on a road trip sometimes.' It was fair to say that, for the first time in months, Jennifer Aniston was happy. Defining happiness, she declared, 'Sunsets make me happy, silly things make me happy. A nice bottle of wine with some good cheese makes me happy.' Right now, Jennifer was in a healthy place. It was time to lift the pause button and move on with the rest of her life.

Chapter 14

Welcome Distractions

Seeking distraction from her private life, Jennifer immersed herself in work. 'It's good to have something creative – an outlet,' she claimed. 'I loved having work to go to. And, when I wasn't working, that was fine too.' Given her current profile, she was never short of offers. Films on the horizon included *Friends With Money*, the Rob Reiner-directed comedy *Rumor Has It*, *Gambit* and *Derailed*. The latter presented Jennifer with yet another opportunity to move away from the comedy roles for which she was famous. The main crux of the movie focused on the absence of honesty and friendship in relationships. Jennifer would play the role of a career woman who seduces married businessman Clive Owen.

It was a curious choice for the actress. 'It was different for me and it was something I was a little hesitant to do, but I love a good thriller,' she explained. After an initial

243

reading of the script, Jennifer decided it was exactly the challenge she required. 'When I read the script, I was thinking, This is one of those movies that I may walk out of going, "Come on now, did we really have to sit through that?" But it's such a great ride. I didn't know it would be this well done, this well written. I read it from beginning to end and just had no clue where it was going next. I like to think I can usually figure out where a story is going.'

Admittedly, Jennifer was nervous about taking on the role. For a while, she wondered if she could really pull it off. But she'd sensed a similar fear when approached with *The Good Girl*. 'That happens with projects that are a little more challenging. It's just a normal process.' Fortunately, her director Mikael Hafstrom had incredible faith in the actress. 'Thank God for directors like him, who can take my persona and put it in a part like this. Whatever my persona is, it's not granted me the opportunity to do roles like this before.'

Another factor in accepting the part also pivoted around Clive Owen's involvement. By a bizarre twist of fate, the Brit actor's name had cropped up in conversation only weeks beforehand. Jennifer took it to be a sign, directing her towards the movie. 'I was in Italy with my ex, while *Ocean's Twelve* was being filmed,' she explained. 'All of us were having lunch at George Clooney's house. I'd just had the script sent to me and I opened the package and it said: *Derailed* starring Clive Owen. I was thinking, Wow, Clive Owen – I love him!, when out of the blue Julia Roberts goes, "Has anybody ever worked with Clive Owen?" It was an omen. I told her about the script and she told me I had to work with him. He's dreamy.'

Once again, Jennifer was stepping into new creative territory. One of the hardest scenes she was required to film involved an attempted rape. But Jennifer insisted the acting experience was in no way traumatic. 'It was very controlled and I was in very good hands. Vincent Cassel is a pro. He has total control of his body so I felt safe. That's very important not to be reckless as an actor. The scene isn't too graphic. But it's very quick and extremely jarring.'

Besides, the atmosphere on set was often reassuringly light-hearted. 'We were always laughing between takes. There were certain moments when, you know, you had to focus more than others, but, even when we were shooting the most emotional scenes, as soon as Mikael, the director, said, "Cut," the mood was immediately light-hearted. And Mikael has a slightly odd and wicked sense of humour, so if anything he was the ringleader.'

Thematically, the film also touched potentially raw nerves. Relating her character's actions to her own experiences in the past year, Jennifer declared, 'Life doesn't make sense sometimes, does it? You can have everything wonderful in the world and you just make stupid choices; because you're bored for a moment or not fulfilled. You can succumb to outside temptation and excitement. This is definitely a film about thinking twice before you do that.' When pushed on the topic of fidelity, Jennifer was slightly more unnerved. 'I think fidelity is very important in a marriage. It's men who usually do the cheating – that's a very general statement, but I'm sure if we did a poll it would turn out that it was more men than women.'

Filming *Derailed* was a cathartic release and Jennifer quickly bonded with her cast mates. Both Jennifer and Clive enjoyed a healthy on-screen chemistry. He even went so far as to compliment Jennifer for being 'as good a dramatic actress as it's possible to be.... No one has seen her do this kind of part before, and it was a very smart choice to book Jennifer in. The bottom line is, she's a really classy actress – incredibly smart and sensitive,' he gushed. 'She was just hugely refreshing, completely unstarry, completely uncomplicated. There was no fuss. With big stars, you never know quite what to expect. But, for somebody who's lived under the spotlight for so long, she's incredibly sorted out and grounded. That was inspiring – that you can be a real human being. It takes an enormous amount of intelligence to keep rooted amidst that glare.'

Jennifer agreed they had both adopted a similar approach to filming. 'It was great!' she smiled. 'It was instant, easy and comfortable. That doesn't always happen.'

Much of the filming took place on location in Chicago. Jennifer fell instantly in love with the windy city. 'Chicago is one of the greatest cities I've ever been to. I've absolutely fallen in love with it,' she enthused. 'People are kind and interesting and interested in other things – they leave you alone – and there are great museums and restaurants.'

Fortunately, Jennifer had a further opportunity to

sample the city during filming for her next movie – the aptly titled *The Break-Up*. Produced and co-written by Vince Vaughn, the film touched on more familiar romantic-comedy terrain. Vince was determined Jennifer should be involved in the project. 'She was always the one we had in mind for Brooke,' he insisted. 'When we rehearsed, I was impressed with her acting and timing. It was also a good role. Unfortunately, a lot of times, women in romantic comedies are stuck sort of rolling their eyes at what the guy does. I wanted her to be really funny on screen, too. Jennifer is the heart of this movie... She's so genuine and funny. You can see why people are so enamoured by her. She's a combination of so many wonderful things. She makes you strive to do better as an actor, as a person.'

At first, Jennifer thought the suggestion was almost laughable – if only because the title was loaded with irony. 'They were all nervous to approach me for the role. But I thought, *The Break-Up*, seize the moment! And it's been great.'

In the movie, Jennifer and Vince play a couple who buy an apartment, split up and have to live together until it's sold. Gary is a tour-bus operator and Brooke is an art-gallery curator. After a year together, they hit a rough spot. She wants him to do the dishes, go to the ballet and love the fact that the new curtains don't allow room for his dream pool table. 'This movie was fate,' laughed Jennifer. 'To be able to walk through a movie called *The Break-Up*, about a person going through a break-up, while I'm actually going through a break-up?! How did that happen?! It's been cathartic. It's turned something into a fantastic experience. Not that divorce is fantastic, but I've never had more fun in a creative process... After reading the script, I thought there was no better way to heal than through laughter. I don't know if I could have done as good a job with it if it had come six months earlier.'

Responsible for co-writing the screenplay, Vince was inspired by the insipidness of the romantic-comedy scripts he was being sent. 'It was the exact same story again and again. Perfect people saying exactly the right thing, always in some kind of magical world... It always had some kind of sub-plot to it: "OK, if you don't marry your girl in six months, you won't inherit my company and I'm going to leave it to the mean guy who works for me". I thought, That's kind of an uptown problem. Relationships are strange enough as it is.'

Eschewing the formulaic norm, he turned to his own personal experiences. 'It's based on elements of my relationships. We've all been here. This is a couple who argue when he brings home three lemons and she told him she needed 12 for a centrepiece. As we all know, they're not really arguing about the lemons. It's *never* about the lemons.'

The director, Peyton Reed (*Bring It On, Down with Love*), described the film as 'a comedy that we tried really hard to ground in reality, so that a lot of the arguments this couple has as they are breaking up are very real. Working opposite Vince, Jen gets to flex her comedic muscles, which are formidable, but she also gets to do a lot of dramatic work in the movie. She just knocked it out of the park.'

A true professional, Jennifer locked out the media madness that was going on around her and gave her complete dedication to the project. 'Had I not gone to the newsstand and seen the tabloids,' said Peyton, 'I would never have known something of that magnitude was going on. She was able to come to work and dig in and just make it a joy every day. Only Jen can speak about her process, but her performance in the movie, when it hits those notes of pain at the end of a relationship, has an immediacy that I was just blown away by.' Jennifer agreed she had given a great performance. 'I love this movie,' she said. 'I have a good feeling about it. It's beautifully balanced and surprisingly emotional. I don't think anyone has really seen anything quite like it.'

By getting into character, Jennifer took time to reflect on her own experiences of relationships – from the daily grind to the deeper emotional ties. 'Well, you might not believe it, but I do the dishes,' she joked. 'In fact, I'm a little crazy about doing them. I'm definitely the type of woman who needs a clean kitchen before I go to bed.' She clearly had issues with household co-operation. 'Some men – there's that chip that tends to be there or tends not to be there – listen. And I think some men are not raised that way, especially with cleaning. I don't know how many men are raised doing dishes. My father – I don't know if he ever did a dish or picked up his clothes. His mother did. And I think women are nurturers. We're caretakers. That's our job.'

But she agreed women often did too much in the home. 'I think that's because it's just instinctual as a woman to be the caretaker of your home. Women complain that men don't do enough, but it's only your own fault. You train your man to do nothing. You can't blame someone then for not knowing what his or her job should be if you don't ask for it right off the bat.'

Equally, working her way through the script enabled Jennifer to understand why not all relationships work out. 'Two people can get lazy, comfortable, and the fantastic things you loved about each other become the things you loathe. And, if you don't deal with it, you lose sight of each other and end up thinking, If only we'd learned how to talk to each other instead of – not even consciously – playing games, we'd still be together. But sometimes you just have to go through things to learn that some relationships aren't going to last forever, that they're meant to teach you big lessons. That's certainly one I've had to learn.

'A romantic relationship can be like nothing else – if only because you put yourself in the uncomfortable position of revealing who you are to another human being,' she continued. 'The point is, married or not, you've got to feel safe with somebody, secure that you can show parts of yourself – dark, light, conscious, unconscious, rational, irrational – and know you're on a safe playing field. A relationship is fifty-fifty. Nobody is always at the top of their game; we all make mistakes.'

While on location in Chicago, Jennifer was accompanied by a bodyguard at all times. 'It's nice to have someone run interference,' she admitted. 'Mostly to protect you from those evil paparazzi vultures – they charge you so that they can get this look of absolute horror – because you're being charged! Then they write some wonderful caption like "Jen, furious!" Whatever happened to, like, hiding in a bush?'

But, soon, Jennifer found herself keeping much better company. Originally from Chicago, Vince Vaughn seized upon the opportunity to show his leading lady around town. The pair were frequently photographed sipping beer in the stands of a baseball stadium. During the day, they explored the city's architecture and at night kicked back with a late-night hot dog at the legendary Weiner's Circle or caught a show at one of the city's smoky jazz clubs. Both actors were in their element. Vince even quit smoking and packed on 25lb!

'I had a blast!' Jennifer beamed. 'I danced more and played more in the last two months than in the last ten years.'

For the most part, they managed to dodge the paparazzi. 'It really wasn't bad because the people of Chicago left us alone,' claimed Vince. 'We even went to a Cubs game and Taste of Chicago. We went to Second City. We went to see Sue the big dinosaur. Let's put a plug in for Sue! That was really cool. It's Chicago. Everyone goes about their business.'

Dramatic changes were taking place. Jennifer couldn't pinpoint exactly when, but all of a sudden men started to fall into her sight path. 'One day, it's like a switch went off, and all of a sudden it was like, Men! Everywhere! The cloud is lifting,' she smiled. 'I'm starting to see the light, and it's good.'

But one man in particular was becoming a regular

fixture in Jennifer's life. While making *The Break-Up*, she and Vince Vaughn had become extremely good friends. Jennifer gushed with words of praise for her co-star. 'He's very funny. He's brilliantly funny. He's hilarious. He's unbelievably ferociously talented and has a work ethic that is inspiring. It was pure fun… We had a ball. He's like working with a pro tennis player. He's so good at his job, plus he's just so funny and he's a great actor. I could just keep volleying to him. He's a really generous actor and likes to try things. I also love to try things. You don't always get that kind of fun and feel like you're on an equal playing field.'

She agreed they enjoyed a fantastic chemistry in front of the camera. The connection had been instant. 'I felt really safe with Vince,' she admitted. 'I felt immediately comfortable, like I had known him for a while. Chemistry is a funny thing. I don't know how you feel it, but you definitely do. It's either there or it's not, and it's pretty clear on either side whether it's present or not.' Professionally, the two actors gelled seamlessly. 'It's great when you can have that thing where you can have a good volley with someone.'

Vince was more than happy to return the compliment. 'She has Elvis dust,' he grinned, in awe of Jennifer's star quality. 'She's the sort of person you could put in a room and all the kids would come over, not even knowing who she is.' He also paid tribute to her unique 'emotional intelligence'. 'People could abuse that. But she chooses to use her gifts to make people feel good. She chooses to be kind, which is, given her situation, really saying something. But, then again, she did once consider becoming a therapist.'

However, there were several logistical problems to overcome. 'With him at six foot five and me at five foot five, they had trouble keeping us in the same frame!' Jennifer giggled. 'I was constantly having to wear these incredibly high heels, which was like having a workout. And sometimes even that wasn't enough. I spent many an hour standing on an apple box.'

The pair had obviously hit it off. But was there a case for life imitating art? Jennifer remained coy. 'He's a good friend,' was all she would say. 'First and foremost he's a really good, loyal friend. Fiercely loyal. He is protective and very loyal to his family and friends. If you're his friend, it's for life, something I respect in a person. In fact, I have a great amount of respect for him in many, many ways.' But she did highlight several enviable qualities that would make the funnyman eligible as boyfriend material. 'Well, he's fantastic. He's a very deep human being, incredibly smart, loves history. He's interested and interesting. He asks questions. It's not just about him.' Jennifer needed no convincing that Vince was a good catch. 'Trust me. He's dreamy,' she grinned.

Jennifer agreed love was the only cure for love, but at her current point in life she wasn't ready for another relationship. 'I'm good right now. I have so much love. I have love. My women friends – they're all my mothers, they're all my sisters, they're all my partners, they're all my wives. It's hard to find a man who can live up to any of them.'

That didn't mean to say Vince was completely out of the running. 'I adore him,' she stressed with overwhelming sincerity. 'He's delicious and funny. He's got all the colours of the rainbow. But I don't want to be a rebound girl. I feel like it will happen when it happens.'

Everyone agreed, however, that Vince was just the tonic Jennifer needed. 'He's one of the funniest guys I've been around,' said Jason Bateman, who played Vaughn's friend in the film. 'She couldn't have picked a better person to spend a few months with while she's going through all this. Vince really looks out for her.'

On the face of it, Vince couldn't be more different to Brad. A much lower-profile celebrity, he was 'sensitive and painfully shy'. By his own admission, he enjoyed blokeish activities such as 'playing video games, that kind of stuff', and was once arrested for defending himself in a bar brawl. Humble to the core, he even made endearing jokes about the benefits of stardom. 'I would give this advice to any single guys out there. This is a piece of gold. If you have the opportunity to star in a movie, do. I find it gets a lot easier to meet girls.'

One thing was for certain, however, Jennifer was still an incurable romantic capable of falling in love. She laid out the conditions for any potential suitors. 'I don't like chocolates. I do love flowers. Anyone who wants to capture my heart can get me some good peonies or orchids. See, I like to hit both price points.' Beyond the superficial, Jennifer counted consideration amongst the key qualities she was seeking. 'I don't need things. People just want to be equal participants. I'd much rather have that than a bouquet of flowers.' And the turn-offs? 'Lying is a no-no. Inconsistency. Those are the two big ones. Any kind of cruel behaviour is not acceptable. A lot falls under that umbrella. Someone who hates dogs.

'I love the human mind, the human emotion, the human being,' she enthused. 'We're fascinating creatures. I love the shadow parts of ourselves and the good parts of ourselves. And only recently have I gotten to that place of learning to embrace all of them – no apologies. My friend and I the other day were like, 'We're gonna rename ourselves the F**kits! You know, "F**k it! Just live."'

Despite events of the past few months, Jennifer would definitely consider marriage again. 'I'll definitely marry again because I believe in it,' she promised, 'though I've done some rethinking on what the institution of marriage means. Maybe I'm old-fashioned: I love the idea of two people declaring their commitment. But look at Goldie Hawn and Kurt Russell, Oprah and Stedman – how well they've done not doing it... My biggest growth spurt was from 34 to 37. Until then, you don't know enough to change. At 25, even 30, you're so tortured and defensive; it's always the other person's fault. Now I just feel so much wiser.'

In press conferences, Vince joked that he would probably make the worst boyfriend in the world. 'I don't like to do the dishes. I do like to watch sporting events. I'm not big on the ballet,' he said, ticking off each finger. 'The absolute worst is I don't care if the new curtains are white or beige. Women should know that most men are less concerned about curtain colour than their mates would like to believe. To be honest, we just want to sign off and have the curtain conversation stop at any cost.' But there were some positives. 'I have two older sisters. I've always gotten along with women. I guess I really enjoy the friendship part of a romantic relationship as much as anything else.'

He joked that filming *The Break-Up* had landed him in a position where he was suddenly qualified to give advice on relationships. 'Suddenly I feel like I'm Dr Phil. I'm saying things like, "Men and women need to give each other space," which by the way is true.'

But he did go on to admit that he was on the market for a woman. 'I know that I need friendship and a sense of humour. I like someone who can make me laugh and laugh at myself. I also need a girl who can roll with life. Life is always about peaks and valleys. The biggest thing for me is having someone where there is a trust, too. It's different when you're younger. Your priorities are different. Now I'm older and in a different place. It's about trust.' It didn't take a genius to see that Jennifer clearly fitted his bill.

The tabloids quickly latched on to Jennifer's supposed relationship with Vince. Ironically, Vince had even made a cameo performance in *Mr & Mrs Smith*, the film that had allegedly destroyed Jennifer's golden marriage. The incestuous circle of intrigue couldn't get any better. A pro at dealing with these sorts of things, Jennifer nonchalantly shrugged off reports. 'You've gotta have goals,' she deadpanned, referring to the persistent paparazzi. 'You gotta have something to do, so you may as well stalk people.'

Her director Peyton Reed commended Jennifer for her ability to block out the nonsense. 'In terms of Jen's attitude at work, I would not have known it was going on because she has this extraordinary ability to shake it off.'

Vince, however, found it less easy to cope. He was an extremely private man and had never been forced to deal with this kind of attention before. Suddenly, he was thrust into the media limelight and he didn't like it one little bit. 'You can't really be like, "Oh, I'm an actor, I'm being followed by the paparazzi and it's horrible." I just think that there's a bounty for a picture, and if that gets higher they're prepared to do more and more,' he said philosophically. 'In the scheme of life, it's ridiculous.'

Refusing to rise to speculation, the couple remained frustratingly vague about the extent of their relationship. They weren't about to give anything away. 'You know, here's my answer to that stuff. I'm not a person who discusses all the ins and outs of what's going on with me *ad nauseam*, because I feel like it betrays something that's mine, that's special to me. It's private, it's my stuff. Ultimately, if people know or don't know it won't change their lives. And it's not out of not being happy about something or proud or excited. It's just not what I do. I've never discussed girls I was dating. I felt that that's a good way to hurt a relationship.'

Jennifer agreed. In the past, she had been too open about her private life and had suffered the consequences. From now on, she would draw a distinct line between her personal and professional life. 'I'm keeping my personal life off the table,' she said. 'All I'll say is that I loved it, I had a great time in Chicago, that's it, that's all. I've learned my lesson, you know what I mean? I'm not going to throw that one up the flagpole and see if anybody salutes... Vince is a fantastic guy, and we're certainly friends, but, as for those silly rumours, we are not engaged, not getting married at Oprah's, not rushing to have a child.'

There was even a suggestion the romantic liaison had been fabricated to boost box-office sales. 'That's not my style with stuff,' quipped Vince.

But Universal Pictures marketing president Adam Fogelson was the first to admit a media buzz had raised the film's profile considerably. 'Just about everyone knows this movie is coming. All the attention that Vince and Jen have gotten over the last many months is substantially responsible.' His hunch was correct. Made for $52 million, the film took an incredible $32,172,785 on its opening weekend.

But Jennifer hoped people would not be drawn to the movie simply because of events in her private life. 'I didn't shoot this movie so that people would go see it because it reflects what's happening in my private life,' she said. 'I'd like to be given a little bit more credit. I know that that's been said, but I don't give a shit what people think. I do parts based on what speaks to me and what I feel I could do a good job at. This just happens to be that.'

One scene that may have pulled in the crowds was Jennifer's nude scene. In an attempt to show Gary what he is missing, Brooke has an intimate waxing (which she refers to as a 'Telly Savalas' – a reference to her real-life famous godfather) and strolls through the flat naked. 'I felt very exposed but I didn't have a choice,' sighed Jennifer. 'He wrote it,' she said, pointing at Vince, 'and I was getting paid... When I first read it, it was so long: "she walks down the hallway, walks in front of the TV, goes to the fridge and gets a cola". I thought, There is no way we can shoot this. This is going to be an NC-17. But they figured out a way to do it very tastefully. It was not gratuitous. But I would never just... I don't walk round my own house naked for that long.'

As for Vince, he was more than happy to sit back and take in the view. 'I thought that was a really easy scene for me,' he laughed. 'It was probably my favourite day of shooting!'

Eventual confirmation of Jennifer's relationship with Vince came when photographs of the couple kissing emerged. But still they refused to discuss the relationship in public. People could make up their own minds. 'You're damned if you do, you're damned if you don't. Everybody will say what they want, whatever – but if I know that I've contributed or haven't contributed to what is bull and what's not bull then I feel better.'

One tabloid suggested the pair had shacked up in the Hollywood hills home Jennifer had purchased years previously. Originally, she had intended to sell the property after moving in with Brad. 'I never sold it. I couldn't let it go,' she confessed. 'I'm living there now.'

But it wasn't quite the idyllic spot she always remembered. In her years of absence a family of marauding bunny rabbits had taken over. 'Those fucking rabbits,' she complained, shaking her head. 'They were cute at first. Look at the bunnies! And now there are 500 of them and you walk on to the grass and it's just crunch, crunch, crunch. There's rabbit shit everywhere. Those bunnies are the bane of my existence. I don't know what they do, how they have the strength to gnaw through the wire we put up to cover the holes. It was like a *National Geographic* out there: the quail, the bunnies, my dog, Norman, killing all the birds.'

But it would take more than a few rabbits to run Jennifer down. After a year of sadness, frustration and humiliation, she had emerged a new woman – on top of her world. Even her friends were amazed by the remarkable transformation. 'Jennifer has done some rebuilding, restructuring and realigning,' said her pal Andrea Bendewald. 'She has come out this beautiful woman standing up tall and happy and full. I thought she was amazing two years ago, but now I look at her and say, "Slow down! You're gonna start levitating soon you're so happy."'

It had taken 12 months of hard work, but at last Jennifer was ready to love again. 'I didn't ever walk out with the intention of "I've got to start dating again",' she insists. 'You just wake up one day and you start to feel like, "Yeah I think I'm open to that now." It's not mapped out. It just sort of happened.' She was looking forward to falling in love again and experiencing the lightheadedness of a romance in its early stages. In the next few years, she was also determined to embrace motherhood. 'Ideally I'd like to have a couple, but who knows? That's part of the unknown that I like.' Her only gripe was that much of her private life would be conducted in public. 'It's just a bummer,' she says. 'It's such a hassle to think that you can't easily and privately fall in love or be courted or anything. But I doubt I have a choice in the matter. It's just something that comes with the dinner.' That said, Jennifer was determined to do everything in her power to keep a new love sacred and safe from prying eyes.

Meanwhile, the rumour mill continued to grind at speed. Were Vince and Jennifer an item? Mumblings of marriage were heard in celebrity circles after Jennifer was reportedly seen sporting a $500,000 9.5 carat canary yellow diamond ring. There were even suggestions Oprah had been employed as a wedding planner. "(The rumors) are so unbelievable," fumed Jennifer in an interview with the TV host. "It sounds like you're giving me Santa Barbara." Asked if she had anything to announce, Jennifer said, "No wedding, no moves, no, no."

Jennifer had also gained a few pounds in recent months, sparking suggestions she might be pregnant. 'No,' she told close friend Oprah Winfrey. 'Here's what it is – this is the funny thing – you're either, "Oh, look at the bump" or "The Pregnant..." and they circle the bump and there's an arrow. But, instead, it's like, you know, maybe a couple of cheese plates too many...' But Jennifer did have a new baby in her life... 'Dolly. A little puppy. A little five-month old. A little white German Shepherd.'

No sooner had Vince and Jennifer been declared an item, however, rumours of a spilt began to circulate. Some suggested Jennifer's celebrity profile too much for the humble funnyman to deal with, while others reported Jennifer had initiated the split because she did not believe Vince was the "marrying kind". Other sources claimed Vince's mother had told her son he would be in for a "world of heartbreak" if he married Jennifer because she had not yet found closure with her ex-husband Brad. Jennifer cleared up any speculation during an interview with Oprah Winfrey. She assured TV audiences that she and Vince had not split – neither were they engaged.

Whilst Vince was in London filming his new project Fred Claus, several tabloids alleged he had been spotted kissing a mystery blonde. Disgusted, he threatened to sue the papers involved. In October 2006 Jennifer came to visit Vince in London. The couple had been apart for two months. They were photographed sightseeing in the city and even took in a matinee performance of the hit musical *Wicked*.

But within a matter of weeks, the couple announced they had officially split. "After Jennifer's trip to London several weeks ago, Jennifer and Vince mutually agreed to end their relationship but continue to be good friends today," their representatives Stephen Huvane and John Pisani told *People* magazine. The couple remained true to their word and Vince was even a guest at Jennifer's 38th birthday party. Vince also showed his support for Jennifer at the People's Choice Awards in January, where the pair each earned trophies for *The Break-Up*. He said of his co-star, "She's awesome. She has just a wonderful warmth and likeability about her."

Impervious to the media circus surrounding her,

Jennifer was eager to move on with her life. Besides men, she had even greater ambitions. Already, she had organised several girlie holidays with her close group of female confidantes. The clan had recently paid a visit to Cabo San Lucas in Mexico. Having come full circle, she was ready to reclaim the idyll as her own. 'I love the sea, I love the sand, I love the water!' she exclaimed, closing her eyes and taking a deep breath. Around her neck, she wore a gold charm necklace with good luck symbols from around the world: an owl, an elephant and a horseshoe. It was a gift from her female friends and a reminder of the charmed life Jennifer was now lucky to lead.

Jennifer was also reunited on-screen with her best friend, when she landed a guest spot on Courteney Cox's new show *Dirt*, a sitcom set in the world of magazine publishing. Jennifer was cast as a lesbian and even enjoyed an on-screen kiss with Courteney! "It's a good-bye kiss!" sighed Jennifer, amazed by the amount of uproar the innocent lip-lock had generated. "I don't honestly think people want to see Rachel and Monica have at it." On reading the script, Jennifer knew the tabloids would have a field day. "I think I won a bet. I told Courteney, "How many days will it take to come out? 'Lesbian kiss! Lip-lock!' " It was a record: about a week." Overall, Jennifer enjoyed the experience. Working with her best friend was like slipping back into a comfortable pair of well-worn slippers. "We had a ball. It was completely fun. I forgot just how much fun we have together in the work world."

In the future, Jennifer was determined to take more

time out and travel the world. Thanks to her period of reflection, she now realised how important it was to stop once in a while. Allow life to pass you by and you might miss it. 'I enjoy travelling and experiencing different places and cultures. The world is such a huge place and so interesting, but it would take lots of lifetimes to get to know it all.' Another hobby Jennifer wished to develop was cooking. 'I can do breakfast and lunch pretty well, but I want to learn how to cook really great dinners. I love the whole thing of cooking and putting together a beautiful table. I love all that stuff.'

There was also the possibility of uprooting and leaving LA. 'There is no Raid that has been invented to get rid of the paparazzi,' she joked. 'But I think it's going to hit a peak, and then it will start to equalise. It just has to. Isn't that sort of the laws or something? Physics? What goes up must come down? I want to get out of here because I walk around and I feel like I should just have the word 'chump' written on my shirt. There's something weird about the energy of this town. Don't you just feel a little film of some kind that coats everything?' But where would she go? 'I don't know. But it also makes sense for me to leave. I can. I don't have a day job. I don't have *Friends* to go to. So I could live outside Los Angeles and fly in for work. That's the freedom of what we do. It's kind of exciting. There's a menu of options.'

Most importantly of all, Jennifer was ready to build a home. 'It's one of my most important things – more important even than doing another movie is creating my home. Whatever that means. Whether it's my family, my friends. Home.'

As for Brad, Jennifer was ready to close that chapter of her life. He was a love she would never forget. But somehow, with time, the pain had gradually subsided. 'In the future. What's ahead. I've learned you can't change somebody. You be what you want to attract to you. You try to live by example and then hopefully it will come to you.' There were certainly lessons to be learned. 'There's a lot I would probably do differently. I wouldn't give over so much of myself. I love taking care of people… but somewhere along the way you sort of lose yourself. I've always been that way in relationships, even with my mom. It's not the healthiest. I feel like I've broken the pattern now. I'll never let myself down like that again. I feel like my sense of self is being strengthened because of it.' Whatever had happened, she had no regrets. 'Just great experiences,' she smiled.

From now on, Jennifer would put herself first. 'That's the only way you can really have a great relationship – if yourself is your priority. You don't compromise yourself. Compromise is such a weird word to use in the context of relationships because it sounds like you're giving up something of yourself. A good friend said it's better to look at it as a collaboration. You should be present, participate, give, nurture and care. Do all of that but still take care of yourself. I don't think it works any other way.'

As for the future, it lay refreshingly open. Rewinding backwards ten years, Jennifer Aniston would never have imagined herself to be in this situation. But that was the beauty of life. It was impossible to predict. Despite having experienced divorce in both her childhood and adult life,

Jennifer still believed in true love. In her lifetime, she'd already experienced highs and lows some people could never dream of. That in itself was a blessing. Over time, she had grown into a contemplative and astute woman.

She had plenty of ambitions, but for the time being she preferred not to elaborate. 'I'm not going to talk about grand dreams, because those are mine, and if I don't fulfil them then I'll be really disappointed that I didn't and that I stood on a soapbox and was like, "I'm going to direct! And I'm going to produce!" That's why I don't make New Year's resolutions. I have a lot that I want to do, though.'

For now Jennifer was ready to embrace the unknown. 'I'm not the sort of person who plans or maps things out. People say, "Where do you see yourself in five or ten years?" I'm very moment to moment and I kind of just trust in that philosophy.' Whatever lay in store, she was determined to enjoy the ride. 'I don't know what will happen next. Isn't that intriguing? Maybe we should all think less and live a little more.'

Jennifer Aniston

The Biography of Hollywood's Sweetheart

Sarah Marshall

JOHN BLAKE

Published by John Blake Publishing Ltd,
3 Bramber Court, 2 Bramber Road,
London W14 9PB, England

www.blake.co.uk

First published in hardback in 2007

ISBN: 978-1-84454-400-4

British Library Cataloguing-in-Publication Data:

A catalogue record for this book is available from the British Library.

Design by www.envydesign.co.uk

Printed in Great Britain by Creative Print and Design, Wales

1 3 5 7 9 10 8 6 4 2

Papers used by John Blake Publishing are natural, recyclable products
made from wood grown in sustainable forests. The manufacturing processes
conform to the environmental regulations of the country of origin.

Every attempt has been made to contact the relevant copyright-holders,
but some were unobtainable. We would be grateful if the appropriate
people could contact us.